HIKING &
BACKPACKING

Karen Berger

B PREPARED

HIKING & BACKPACKING

Karen Berger

DK

DK

LONDON, NEW YORK, MUNICH, MELBOURNE, DELHI

Project Editor	Steve Setford
Art Editor	Peter Radcliffe
Project Manager	Nigel Duffield
Publisher	Sophie Mitchell
Mike Vaccaro	Director of Business Development
Brian Saliba	Business Development Manager

This is an abridged and revised edition of *Eyewitness Companion* produced for Dorling Kindersley by **The Bridgewater Book Company Ltd**

First American Edition, 2007

Published in the United States by
DK Publishing, Inc.
375 Hudson Street,
New York, New York 10014

07 08 09 10 11 10 9 8 7 6 5 4 3 2 1

A Cataloging-in-Publication record for this book is available from the Library of Congress.

ISBN 978-0-7566-3522-0

DK books are available at special discounts for bulk purchases for sales promotions, premiums, fund-raising, or educational use. For details, contact: DK Publishing Special Markets, 375 Hudson Street, New York, NY 10014 or SpecialSales@dk.com

Color reproduction by GRB Editrice, Italy
Printed and bound in China by L. Rex Printing Co. Ltd.

Discover more at
www.dk.com

Introduction 6

Chapter One
CLOTHING AND EQUIPMENT

CONTENTS

HIKING IS ABOUT ENJOYING YOURSELF. Whether you choose to hike close to home or further afield, you can find a host of trails that will lead you to areas of natural beauty. The combined pleasures of rhythmic walking, beautiful scenery, the sun on your back, and a path stretching away from you are what make hiking so popular.

Walking is one of the most effective forms of exercise. Being low impact, it is suitable for virtually everyone. When undertaken at a brisk pace it provides good aerobic exercise, tones your muscles, and improves your general physical condition. Start with easy walks on level ground, then build your fitness by hiking in the hills, where the terrain will make you push yourself a bit harder. Eventually, you may be able to tackle a mountain.

Cars and trains can take you to many wonderful places, but parking the car or getting off the train, and setting out on a footpath enables you to see many places that lie off the beaten track, away from well-traveled tourist routes. You will see the area more intimately than most visitors, and visit tiny villages, hidden beaches, and secret waterfalls.

As a hiker you will be exposed to the weather, with no car window or air-conditioning between you and nature. If it is sunny, you will probably get hot; if it is windy, you may be blown around; and if it rains, you will get wet. But being out in the elements appeals to most hikers, who relish just being outside—whatever the conditions. You will also be closer to wildlife, enjoying the sights and sounds of birds and animals in their natural environment. Nature reserves and trails in remote areas are especially good places to experience wildlife without the intrusions of modern-day life.

Hiking can be a very sociable activity. Whether you go for a day or a month, hiking offers an opportunity to spend uninterrupted time with friends and family, exploring new places together. If you enjoy the social side of hiking, choose a popular trail where hikers congregate in shelters, huts, lean-tos, or designated camping areas. You often find these on long distance

paths, such as the Appalachian Trail. Alternatively, you can join a hiking club and go on a group hike.

If you prefer to treat hiking as quiet, personal time, then travel with one or two carefully chosen companions. You and your friends can choose your own route, camp and eat where and when you want, and be as spontaneous as you like. You can even explore remote, uninhabited areas, following cross-country routes you design yourselves.

Experienced hikers can read maps in thick fog, stay warm and dry in an all-day downpour, cross rough terrain, set up camp quickly in a sudden storm, find food and water in tough conditions, and deal with a host of other difficult situations. Acquiring such skills will not only improve your safety and comfort when hiking, but also ensure that your trip is as memorable and adventurous as you want it to be.

CLOTHING AND EQUIPMENT

Choosing gear

With thousands of items to choose from, your first visit to an outdoor retailer's store may be confusing. Choosing gear is not about buying the latest, most fashionable, or even the most expensive equipment, it is all about buying affordable equipment that matches your needs.

Narrowing the choices

Start by evaluating the weather and terrain you will encounter on your hike, then consider what is—and is not—essential. A tight budget may restrict your choices, but you will still find many functional and practical choices in all price ranges. Do not be seduced by things that you may never use—focus instead on solid gear that meets the needs you have identified.

SETTING GOALS

Understanding your hiking goals will make it easier to choose the right gear for your trip.

ARE YOU HIKING SOLO OR AS PART OF A GROUP?

Solo hiking can be as lightweight and spontaneous as you like, but group hikes mean larger tents, more cooking equipment, and careful planning.

HOW MUCH DISTANCE DO YOU PLAN TO COVER?

For long-distance hikes, keep your pack weight low and only carry what is truly necessary.

WHAT WILL WEATHER CONDITIONS BE LIKE?

Weather reports will determine whether you need light or heavy clothing and gear.

DO YOU HAVE ANY SPECIALIST INTERESTS?

If you are an eager bird-watcher or photographer, you will need to consider the extra weight of binoculars or a camera.

MAKING A CHECKLIST

To make sure you do not carry too much, keep a checklist of the gear that you take. After each hike, make a note of what you did and did not use, then alter your gear list accordingly. (You should always carry emergency equipment such as raingear and a first-aid kit.) Your checklist may change from hike to hike, as you encounter different conditions or as you gain experience. It will become a gear log, in which you make notes about the conditions and how well your gear worked. For example, if you slept

UNSETTLED WEATHER
In changeable climates, you need head-to-toe raingear for safety and comfort in case of a sudden downpour. Pack your gear in a waterproof backpack to ensure that it remains dry.

comfortably on a sub-freezing night in a particular sleeping bag while wearing certain items of clothing, the next time you go out in similar conditions, you will know exactly what to bring. Likewise, you might make a note of items you wished you had—for example, a thicker sleeping mat, a rain hat, or gloves. Also note how much you used of items such as sunscreen, stove fuel, and insect repellent—next time, you might be able to manage with less.

STREAMLINING YOUR GEAR

The following five strategies will help you to keep down the weight and size of your gear. Follow them sensibly and your pack weight will drop without compromising safety.

■ You can easily get rid of excess and cut several pounds from your load by closely examining the contents of your pack. Do not bring extra changes of clothing—instead, rinse clothes in a stream. Also, trim your cooking kit to bare essentials—a single cooking pot will often do.

■ When hiking with a partner, assess what gear you can conveniently share. You can save several pounds by sharing a tent, stove, cooking kit, first-aid kit, pocketknife, and even personal items such as a toilet trowel, sunscreen, and insect repellent.

■ Consider weight when replacing old equipment. Look for newer lightweight components such as siliconized nylon and titanium, and also for simple designs that succeed in maximizing function while minimizing weight.

■ Some equipment can do several jobs, which makes it weight-efficient. For example, a trekking pole helps you to walk during the day and can be used as a tarpaulin support at night. Similarly, a foam mat can be folded to make a backpack frame during the day and then used as a mattress at night.

■ Measure out portions of all consumables. Buy insect repellent in small plastic bottles, or use insect repellent that has built in sunscreen. Travel- or sample-sized soap, toothpaste, and first-aid ointments are lighter than standard sizes. Pack spices in miniature zip-locking bags (available at many food stores) and minimize all packaging (such as cardboard food boxes).

WEIGHT GUIDELINES

Hiking gear comes in a wide range of weights. In average hiking conditions in a temperate climate, keep within the guidelines below for a comfortable trip.

ITEM	MAX. WEIGHT
Backpack	4½ lb (2 kg)
Two-person tent	5½ lb (2.5 kg)
Sleeping bag	2¼ lb (1 kg)
Hiking boots	2¼ lb (1 kg)
Solo tent	3 lb (1.3 kg)
Sleeping mat	1½ lb (650 g)
Raingear (jacket and pants)	1¼ lb (550 g)
Food (per day, per person)	2 lb (900 g)

HIKING LIGHT
You can travel more quickly and cover greater distances with a lightweight backpack.

Clothing

Today's outdoor clothing is technologically advanced and highly sophisticated—new materials and designs are extremely lightweight, durable, and versatile. To make the most of your gear, choose the fabrics and combinations of clothes appropriate to the conditions.

Layering clothes

The rule of layering is simple—it is better to choose several light layers than one heavy layer. Wearing multiple layers gives you the flexibility to fine-tune exactly how warm you are by taking off and putting on layers as you work harder, as you rest, or as the temperature changes. Choose fabrics such as wool, microfleece, fleece, or down, which are good insulators.

HOW LAYERING WORKS

Layering is effective because it traps air between the clothing layers, which means that you stay warm. If you wear the correct layers in the correct order, your clothing will move sweat away from your body, keep moisture out, and insulate you. Wear wicking fabrics in both hot and cold weather.

Lightweight, fitted gloves worn under bulkier fleece gloves protect fingers from the wet and cold

The base layer provides warmth and wicks moisture away from your skin

The mid-layer provides warmth. Use insulating fabrics in cold weather, or when resting in camp

The outer layer of waterproof, breathable fabric keeps rain out and allows water vapor from sweat to escape

Raindrops are repelled

Perspiration is drawn away from the skin

Gore-tex® outer layer

Fleece mid-layer

Synthetic mesh or lightweight layer

Polypropylene base layer

Skin

Heat

Wicking long underwear worn under a protective outer layer gives legs extra warmth

Two pairs of socks can be worn under boots. A lightweight inner sock draws moisture away from feet and lessens friction

LAYERING SYSTEM
The top (outer) layer repels rainwater, while dampness is wicked away. The lower layers retain body warmth.

FABRIC	PROPERTIES	USES
COTTON Comfortable for temperate climates, cotton absorbs water and dries slowly, so is less suitable for cool or wet climates.	■ *Absorbs water* ■ *Provides ventilation*	■ Shorts ■ Pants ■ T-shirts ■ Bandanas ■ Sun-protection hats
WOOL A good insulator, wool next to the skin can be itchy. Merino and cashmere are lightweight, warm for their weight, and do not itch.	■ *High water repellency* ■ *Warm when wet*	■ Socks ■ Sweaters ■ Hats ■ Gloves ■ Long underwear
SILK Though comfortable and lightweight, silk retains moisture. Because of this, it has lost ground to newer, faster-drying synthetics.	■ *Comfortable against skin* ■ *Lightweight*	■ Long underwear ■ Sleeping bag liners
POLYPROPYLENE Both inexpensive and warm, polypropylene wicks moisture away from the skin, keeping you warm, dry, and comfortable.	■ *Wicks moisture away* ■ *Dries quickly*	■ Long underwear ■ Raingear ■ Ski masks ■ Gloves ■ Hats ■ Insulating shirts
FLEECE A bulky, lightweight fabric, fleece keeps you warm. Microfleece is a tighter weave, and weighs less, but is not quite as warm.	■ *Retains warmth when wet* ■ *Warm for weight*	■ Vests ■ Hats ■ Gloves ■ Pants ■ Jackets ■ Ski masks
MICROFIBER A stretchy, tightly woven fiber that allows clothing to fit tightly to the body, microfiber repels wind and some moisture.	■ *Tightly woven* ■ *Repels moisture*	■ Vests ■ Wind jackets ■ Shorts ■ Raingear ■ Towels
GORE-TEX® A water-repellent coating and microscopic holes in Gore-tex® fabrics prevent moisture from entering while allowing sweat to escape.	■ *Coating repels water* ■ *Breathable*	■ Rain jackets ■ Rain pants ■ Gloves ■ Hats ■ Gaiters ■ Boot linings
SOFT-SHELL Similar to an insulating fleece, soft-shell offers excellent breathability, but is inadequate protection in a heavy storm.	■ *Some water repellency* ■ *Good breathability*	■ Jackets ■ Water resistant leggings

Clothes for hot weather

Hiking can be hard exercise that raises your body temperature and can make you uncomfortable. In very warm weather, it is vital to stay as cool as possible to avoid heat exhaustion and possibly heatstroke—and to enjoy yourself. Your choice of clothing can help. Choose breathable fabrics, which will keep you cool while protecting your skin from the heat of the sun.

COPING WITH THE HEAT

Too much exposure to direct sunlight can cause sunburn and dehydration. If you are hiking in very warm weather, pay special attention to your body temperature and make sure you stay hydrated. Heat rashes can also be exacerbated if sweat is not able to evaporate properly.

HOT WEATHER CLOTHING

Protect your skin by covering as much of your body as you can with a thin layer of clothing. Remember to wear a hat as well.

SUN PROTECTION

Clothing should be loose and light-colored to protect your skin from sun and insects.

Synthetic materials wick away moisture and dry more quickly than cotton

Sleeves should be loose so they can be rolled up and secured by a button

A shirt with ventilation flaps allows air to circulate, helping sweat to escape

Check that zippers have a fabric flap inside so they do not chafe your skin

Waterproof boot linings are not necessary in warm weather, particularly in dry climates

KEEPING COOL

Your choice of clothing should help you to keep cool when hiking in the heat and humidity.

A loose fitting t-shirt made from moisture-wicking fabric is good for air flow and comfort

A wide brim shades the face and neck. Light colors reflect the sun's rays

Convertible pants
Lightweight, full-length pants shade the skin from blazing sun. Convertible pants have legs that can be unzipped for those who prefer hiking in shorts

HOT, RAINY WEATHER

You might not need full raingear on a summer hike, so take a water-resistant wind shirt or lightweight rain jacket to protect you from a shower.

WIND SHIRT

This type of shirt is not waterproof but it is water-resistant, which may be sufficient in light summer rain and for the cool nights that usually follow hot days in the desert.

WIND PROTECTION

A wind shirt is useful in warm deserts where strong, dry, seasonal winds are common.

A high collar protects the neck

Tightly woven wind shirt fabrics keep out wind and some water

LIGHTWEIGHT RAIN JACKET

In hot, rainy conditions, an inexpensive rain jacket made of polypropylene is an excellent choice, as it is breathable as well as waterproof. An ultralight jacket will fold away to a tiny pack size.

RAIN PROTECTION

Look for loose-fitting, well-ventilated, lightweight jackets. A breathable fabric allows sweat to escape.

All rain jackets should have a hood. Some have a peak in the front, which helps keep water off the face

Underarm zippers, which are an advanced feature, and a loose fit ensure good ventilation

Lightweight fabrics can tear easily, so take care when rock scrambling or hiking through vegetation

HATS FOR THE HEAT

Hats protect your head and neck from both the sun's rays and insects. They also absorb sweat.

BASEBALL CAP

The wide brim of a baseball cap shelters the eyes from the sun.

BANDANA

A bandana can be rinsed in cool water and worn on top of the head, or worn under a baseball cap to shade the neck.

DESERT HAT

A desert hat combines the sheltering brim of a baseball cap with the neck protection of a bandana.

LIGHTWEIGHT RAIN HAT

A lightweight rain hat gives protection from both sun and rain, so is a good choice for tropical regions.

Clothes for wet weather

Sudden downpours can occur just about anywhere and most hikers have been accidentally caught out in rainstorms or monsoons. Many regions that offer attractive hiking may experience periods of unsettled weather. If you carry the gear necessary to stay warm and dry, and make sure you keep it dry and accessible, you will be prepared for any wet conditions.

FABRICS THAT KEEP OUT MOISTURE

Garments that are breathable and waterproof keep out moisture while allowing sweat to escape. Gore-tex® is the best known of such laminates and used in many outdoor products. Polypropylene is also used to make inexpensive raingear that is both waterproof and breathable.

DRESSING FOR WET WEATHER

Choose raingear that fits loosely enough to allow free movement and to accommodate insulating layers if necessary.

Fleece layer Synthetic down layer Waterproof shell

Synthetic wicking underwear Synthetic or wool shirt

LAYERING IN WINTER

Wearing layers of clothes in cold and wet winter weather will help to keep you both warm and dry.

Gore-tex® laminate Raindrops repelled Jacket shell

Jacket lining Perspiration escapes

BREATHABLE LAMINATES

The tiny holes in Gore-tex® laminate allow droplets of perspiration to escape, while keeping raindrops out.

A breathable, waterproof jacket allows sweat to escape while keeping rain out

Hood keeps the rain off and your neck warm

Rain leggings are essential in cold weather

LIGHT PONCHO

Ponchos, usually made from inexpensive coated nylon, are useful in warm weather because they provide plenty of ventilation. The back of a poncho can be draped over a backpack or daypack as a rain cover.

A hood retains heat around the head and neck

Drawstring fastening keeps the rain out

PONCHO

Choose the lightest poncho available. Very thin ponchos may not last for more than a season, but are worth buying because they are lightweight and inexpensive. They allow free movement and can accommodate extra layers underneath if needed.

Waterproof case
A waterproof map case is essential for navigating in rain.

RAIN HAT

The hat shown has a wide brim, which will prevent water from dripping onto the face and down the back of the neck.

A chin strap will keep a rain hat from blowing off in a strong wind

KEEPING COOL AND DRY

In warm weather, a rain hat will keep your head dry, allow the neck to be ventilated, and also offer protection from the sun.

KEEPING RAINGEAR ACCESSIBLE

Always pack your raingear where you can retrieve it quickly if there is a sudden downpour. Keeping it in a side pocket or front compartment avoids having to open the main pack, which avoids letting in rain.

Multiple compartments allow you to organize your raingear

DAYPACK CHOICE

This should be big enough to hold lunch, emergency gear, essentials, and an extra layer of clothing.

Contents kept inside a drawstring pouch are easily accessible when the weather turns bad

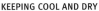

CHOOSING GEAR FOR DIFFERENT CONDITIONS

For warm weather, good conditions, or light showers:
- Lightweight rain jacket or poncho
- Wind shirt
- Loose fitting t-shirt
- Rain/sun hat
- Water-resistant footwear

For cold weather, difficult conditions, or downpours:
- Insulating layers
- Waterproof jacket with hood
- Waterproof leggings
- Gaiters
- Boots
- Rain hat

Clothes and gear for cold weather

Hiking in cold weather can be both exhilarating and enjoyable. There are fewer insects than in hot weather and you are not subject to the debilitating exhaustion resulting from steep climbs in high temperatures. Usually, fewer people are out walking, so you can appreciate the solitude. But to enjoy yourself, you need clothes and equipment that suit the conditions.

SNOWY WEATHER

Use a lightweight base layer to wick away moisture from your skin, several layers of warm insulating clothing, and an outer shell that is waterproof and windproof. You can also use a layering system for your hands. Insulating gloves made of fleece or polypropylene provide warmth, while outer mittens made of a waterproof, breathable fabric keep out moisture. Thin liner gloves allow you to do delicate tasks such as operating a stove or putting tent poles together.

Be sure to brush snow off your clothing, so that it does not creep inside, where it will melt. Walk at a slow, steady pace that you can maintain—this will avoid the need to stop—and get cold.

HIKING IN SNOW

When active in cold conditions, wear a waterproof outer layer to keep warm and dry.

A warm hat is essential. Some wool hats are lined with waterproof, breathable fabric

An external waterproof, breathable layer will keep snow away from your insulating layers

Gloves should have an inner insulating layer and an outer waterproof, breathable layer

Waterproof pants are the protective outer layer, usually worn over wicking or insulating leggings

For extra protection, gaiters cover your boots and keep snow away from your feet

Heavy leather boots will keep your feet warm and dry

SUNGLASSES

It is vital to wear sunglasses in snow, especially above the treeline. Use glacier glasses, which filter out UV light and have side panels that prevent the strong sunlight and harmful rays from coming in at the sides. In very windy weather, snowgoggles offer better protection as they cover more of the face.

Lenses must filter out UV rays

Snug, flexible frames will keep glasses in place during movement

ICE AX

Because you can use it to cut steps in the icy surface as you go, an ice ax is necessary when crossing steep slopes. You can also use it to perform an ice-ax arrest if you start to slip. You may need an ice ax in summer if you are hiking at high elevations in snow-covered terrain. If you expect to need an ice ax, it is best to learn how to use it at a class before you set off.

The curved pick set with teeth can be used as a brake

Sharp spike used to plunge the ax into snow for stability, balance, and safety

INSTEP CRAMPONS

Modified crampons help you to keep your footing on slippery slopes at only a fraction of the weight of fully fledged climber's crampons. Instep crampons fit just under the instep of the boot.

Straps around the boot hold the crampon in place

Instep crampons usually have four points, which dig into the ice

TRACTION DEVICES

Consisting of small metal grips coiled around a rubber-blend web that stretches over the sole of your boot, traction devices act like studded snow tires. They are designed for moderately icy trails, not dangerous mountain slopes, so do not use them in place of crampons.

Removable strap fits over the top of your boot for greater stability

A rubber strap goes under the boot

Studs grip the snow

COOL AND COLD DRY WEATHER

Be sure to wear a wicking base layer to keep moisture away from your skin. When the weather is dry but blustery, use a windproof outer layer (either a wind shirt or a windproof microfiber) to help stay warm. Keep a hat and gloves handy in case the temperature drops further. The secret to staying comfortable is to constantly adjust your layers as your body temperature changes. When you are going uphill and working hard, remove layers to avoid sweating. When you are walking easily downhill, add a layer to stay warm.

A hat helps you regulate your body temperature

Wicking base layers come in several different weights; colder temperatures require heavier weights

A windproof outer layer will help you to stay warm, especially in exposed surroundings

DRESSING FOR THE COLD

Use multiple layers so you can quickly adapt to changing temperatures.

COOL AND COLD RAINY WEATHER

Wear a wicking base layer next to the skin, and an outer layer consisting of a waterproof, breathable jacket and pants. In very exposed conditions where you encounter cold, wind-driven rain, you may need to add another insulating layer to keep your body warm. Most hikers chill quickly in cold weather when they are not walking, so the fewer breaks you take, the better. Try to set a moderate pace that you can keep up all day, even going uphill.

A hood can be worn over a hat for extra protection, if necessary

Draw cords prevent warm air from escaping from the vulnerable neck area

A rain jacket needs to cover the hips and fit over insulating layers

DRESSING FOR THE COLD AND WET

Do not overdress— sweat can soak you as much as rain.

Footwear

Choosing suitable footwear involves matching your needs to one of the many different styles available. Hiking footwear ranges from lightweight trekking sandals to fully fledged mountaineering boots. However, by far the most important factor is a correct fit.

Understanding footwear

Choosing the right boot may be the most important decision you make when selecting gear. An ill-fitting boot can cause nothing but misery, and more hikes are ruined by blisters and foot pain than by anything else. Evaluate the conditions in which you plan to hike, and also consider your own history of footwear use, footwear problems, and fit difficulties.

THE ANATOMY OF A BOOT
Understanding the ways in which the different types of boots are constructed, and the importance—and relevance—of all the different features, means that you can choose the boots that will most suit the conditions in which you plan to hike.

Cushioning pads absorb shock

Heel insert cushions foot

Midsole

Heel cup cradles the midsole

Insole stabilizes the foot and holds it in position

Full-length shank plate adds rigidity

Outsole

A soft collar cushions and supports the ankle, and helps to prevent pebbles and dirt from entering between the foot and the boot

Grommets allow you to adjust the boot around the ankle area

Ankle-height upper provides support without restricting movement

ANATOMY OF A SOLE
A boot sole has several layers, which protect and support your feet. Look for good tread on the outsole, and cushioning beneath the heel and toe areas.

Lining (not visible) is breathable and moves moisture away from the foot

External leather may be waterproofed and is abrasion-resistant

Combined fabric and leather construction makes this boot light, comfortable, and breathable. This type of upper is less likely to cause blisters because it is flexible

Midsole connects the outsole to the upper and gives the boot stability

Outsole, which has deep indentations, gives good grip on slippery surfaces

BOOT CARE

With proper care and regular cleaning, a pair of boots can last for years:

■ Treat leather boots with an appropriate waterproofing solution.

■ Brush, wipe, or rinse off dirt and mud; use boot-cleaning liquid on stubborn grime.

■ Wipe the inner lining of your boots to remove dirt and salt from perspiration.

■ Sprinkle baking soda inside boots to help control odors.

■ Remove laces and insoles from wet boots, stuff the boots with newspaper, and dry them slowly at room temperature. Fast drying boots by a radiator or fire will damage them.

FINDING THE PERFECT FIT

Shop for boots in the afternoon, when your feet are naturally slightly swollen from walking. Wear the socks you plan to wear while trekking. Be sure to have your feet measured while you sit and stand. Alert the salesperson to any problems or fit issues, such as a common blister point.

The boot should fit snugly. With your foot all the way forward, you should be able to fit one finger between the back of your foot and the boot. The forefoot must be wide enough for your toes to move.

Stand on a slope (most shops can provide this) to check that your toes do not bang against the front of the boot when you are facing downhill. When facing uphill, push your heel up as far as it will go. It should not come up more than about $1/2$ in (1 cm). Try on several pairs of boots for comparison. Wear the boots in the shop for a while to feel for any trouble spots, such as rubbing, squeezing, or tingling.

At home, wear the boots indoors for a few days to continue to check the fit. Most retailers let you return boots if you have not worn them outside. When you are happy with your boots, start breaking them in, on short walks at first, then on longer ones. You can adjust your footwear by adding insoles, heel pads, or sockliners.

CHOOSING SOCKS

The function of socks is to wick sweat away from your feet, and to provide cushioning and warmth. They can also be used to fine-tune the fit of a boot. Wear a thicker sock with a slightly large boot, a thinner sock with a slightly tight boot, or two pairs of socks if there is room.

WICKING SOCKS

A lightweight inner sock made from a wicking fabric draws moisture away from your feet, helping to prevent blisters. Lightweight wool and polypropylene socks also do not cause friction, so they are less likely to rub.

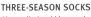

SUMMER-WEIGHT SOCKS

These are thick under the sole and heel, but lighter and thinner around the ankle and over the top of the foot. They are made of wool or a wool-nylon blend. Wool draws moisture away from the foot and provides cushioning. Socks that contain nylon will last longer.

THREE-SEASON SOCKS

Also called trekking socks, three-season socks are thicker than summer-weight socks. They are a good choice for long-distance hikers because their added cushioning is highly effective in preventing blisters.

WINTER-WEIGHT SOCKS

Like other wool socks, these should be worn with a lightweight wicking inner sock. Be sure your boots are big enough to accommodate them. Socks that are too thick for the boot can constrict circulation. Winter socks are only needed in temperatures well below freezing.

Types of footwear

There are two factors that determine the type of boot you select. The first concerns your personal requirements. These include the shape of your feet and how much support they need.

You also need to consider how far you are traveling and the terrain. Keep the weight of your boots as light as possible because unnecessary weight on your feet can be extremely tiring.

DECIDING BETWEEN BOOTS AND SHOES

When deciding whether to wear boots or shoes, choose shoes if you are prone to blisters, if you will be hiking on easy terrain or well-maintained footpaths, or if you will be carrying only a daypack. Wear boots if your ankles are prone to twisting, if you will be hiking cross-country or on rocky or muddy terrain, or if you will be carrying a heavy pack.

TREKKING SANDALS

The traditional amphibious sandal worn by kayakers has recently been adapted for hiking on warm days. Some models have toe bumpers to protect toes from rocks and roots, straps to hold the foot in place, and arch supports to keep the sandal in position. They have rugged soles to grip the trail surface and a strong construction.

Straps hold the foot in place, even on rough terrain

TREKKING SHOE

This type of shoe is lightweight, durable, and usually made of breathable material. Trekking shoes are often less expensive than hiking boots, and provide good traction and lateral support on a variety of terrain. They are often adequate for day hikers or overnight hikers with light backpacks.

A stiff footbed and sole help prevent the foot from twisting

LIGHTWEIGHT BOOT

Fabric and leather hybrids are a good choice for day and overnight hikers on moderate terrain because they combine the support and traction of a boot with the weight and flexibility of a sports shoe. Many have waterproof, breathable linings. These boots tend to cause fewer blisters because of their flexible construction.

Flexible fabric uppers allow the boot to breathe

MIDDLEWEIGHT BOOT

A good compromise between the lightweight boots and the traditional heavier, higher-cut leather boots, middleweight boots are cut lower on the ankle, are made of lighter-weight materials, and are more flexible than traditional leather. They give more support and water repellency than a hybrid.

The boot is cut lower on the ankle than a heavyweight boot, making it more flexible

TRADITIONAL HEAVY LEATHER BOOT

Heavier boots have fallen out of favor with the arrival of new, lighter types. However, they are frequently preferred by hikers who carry heavy loads on rough terrain. Three-season full-grain leather boots provide excellent support and good protection in snow.

A high cut gives good ankle support

SNOWSHOEING BOOT

Traditional snowshoeing boots are lined with thick felt. To reduce heatloss through the sole of the boot, most modern boots have an insulated footbed made of felt or a synthetic material such as Thinsulate®. The waterproof leather upper and rubber outsole keep feet warm and dry.

Flexible uppers are comfortable, but do not give enough support for long hikes

Rubber soles have good traction and there are no seams where water can seep in

CLIMBING AND HIKING HYBRID

Modern climbing boots have a more flexible construction than traditional boots. They are designed to be worn with crampons and to keep feet warm in very cold temperatures, but they can also be worn without crampons for hiking on approach trails. Their weight and stiffness make them inappropriate choices for very long-distance treks.

Crampons can be worn to give extra grip when walking on snow and ice

JUNGLE-TREKKING BOOT

These are high boots made with rubber soles, leather toes, and heels, with canvas and nylon uppers. They should fit sufficiently snugly that the suction of thick mud cannot pull them off your feet. Jungle boots can cause the feet to sweat and swell, so make sure they are not too tight, and wear moisture-wicking socks. In hot weather, carry alternative footwear such as light sports shoes or trekking sandals for camp and for use on easier terrain.

High uppers keep mud off your pants

Leather provides waterproofing

Backpacks

Whether on a day hike or a week-long trek, you will be probably be wearing a backpack, so choosing the right one for your equipment and your body is important. The backpack is one of your most essential items of hiking gear, and it needs to fit comfortably.

Choosing a backpack

A backpack is basically a fabric sack attached to a frame. The sack holds the equipment while the frame distributes the weight. An internal frame is lightweight and comfortable.

External frame backpacks are used by hikers with heavy loads. Daypacks can be used for short hikes. Modular packs give you the flexibility of a large backpack, a holdall, and a daypack.

TYPES OF PACK

Backpacks come in a variety of sizes and styles, all with different features. In North America, pack size is usually measured in cubic inches. Your pack size depends on how long you will be hiking, the climate, how much gear you take, and your body size. A large pack is between 4,500 to 6,000 cubic inches.

EXTERNAL FRAME BACKPACK

These backpacks are the classic hiking carry-alls. Essentially, they consist of a rigid frame, usually made of aluminum, that rides on your back. Suspended from the frame is a sack, normally divided into several compartments. Additional gear can be strapped on the frame, usually above and below the main compartment.

Top compartment is ideal for raingear

Additional compartment makes items accessible

Side pockets for daily necessities

Sleeping bag compartment

Strong, lightweight frame

Hour-glass Shape of frame allows weight to sit high on the back

Hip belt attached to lower frame

INTERNAL FRAME BACKPACK

This type of pack has its origins in the mountaineering world, where an external frame would be a dangerous liability because it could catch on rock or ice. Most of your gear rides securely inside an internal frame backpack, although some expedition packs have external ice ax loops, crampon guards, ski pockets, and lashing points for carrying extra gear.

Additional compartment makes items accessible

Lashing points for extra gear

Top lid compartment, ideal for raingear

Compression strap to reduce bulk

Fully adjustable harness for support

Padded shoulder strap for comfort

Fully adjustable hip belt

Straps for lashing extra items

MODULAR BACKPACK

Modular packs represent a new innovation in backpack design. These packs can be expanded depending on your trip. Take off the daypack if you do not need it, so that you have a smaller, lighter pack on a summer hike. Re-attach it for a longer trip.

Pack can be carried like a duffle bag, using the handle on its side

Main pack is big enough for weekend jaunts

Zip-off daypack can be used separately

LIGHTWEIGHT BACKPACK

A lightweight backpack does not have a rigid frame, so it is easy to travel with it packed inside a suitcase. These backpacks are used by hikers with light loads, and are convenient if you are traveling by train or car, but want the option of taking a hiking trip as well.

Top compartment folds over and is secured with compression straps

Belts on lightweight packs are less padded than belts on standard packs

A frameless pack is light and flexible, but heavy loads may be uncomfortable

BACKPACK FEATURES

Consider these factors when choosing between an internal frame or an external one.

INTERNAL FRAME

■ Carries load weight low and closer to the back
■ Ideal for rough terrain because close fit reduces bouncing and helps to maintain balance
■ Preferred by women because the low center of gravity makes the weight more comfortable

EXTERNAL FRAME

■ Carries weight high up
■ Good for ventilation as frame holds pack away from the back
■ Often less expensive than comparable internal frame packs
■ More compartments for organizing gear

DAYPACK

Carrying a full-size backpack on a day hike is pointless—the pack would be only half full and the extra weight of the bag would be an unnecessary burden. Instead, choose a daypack. Make sure it can carry a full day's supplies for hiking in challenging terrain with unsettled weather. A small daypack need not have a hip belt; but those meant for heavier loads should have one.

Elastic cord strapping can be used to attach items to the outside of the pack

Side pouch can be used to carry a water bottle

Second zipped compartment helps you keep gear organized

STUFF SACKS AND BELT BAGS

Drawstrings close bag

A stuff sack is useful for short, impromptu side-trips from a base camp. The straps used on some compression sacks can also be used to carry the sack over the shoulder knapsack-style. When day-hiking in warm weather with minimal equipment, a belt bag is ideal. It is big enough for snacks and personal items, but not to carry extra clothes such as raingear.

STUFF SACK

Pull up on the straps to compress the bag

BELT BAG ON WAIST

Fitting and packing your backpack

How comfortable a backpack is depends on how well it fits, how well it is packed, and how much it weighs. Packs come in different sizes, with components such as hip belts, harnesses, and frames, so be sure to allow time for fitting when buying. Aim for a pack that rides comfortably on your back without chafing, hurting your shoulders, or pulling on your neck.

MEASURING PACK SIZE

Backpack sizing is based on torso length, which runs from the bony protrusion at the base of your neck to the small of the back. Each manufacturer has its own sizing scale, with some offering different sizes of shoulder harnesses and hip belts.

FITTING YOUR PACK

Fitting should be done with a lightly loaded pack. Shops often have pillows and sacks on hand for this purpose.

Loosen all the straps, fit the pack onto your shoulders, then tighten the lower shoulder straps and the hip belt until they feel snug. You can alter the load lifter straps (behind your shoulders) to transfer weight from the shoulders to the hips and vice versa. Some packs have load stabilizer straps, which pull the backpack more tightly on the hips. Women in particular find this a useful adjustment to make for comfort because of their lower center of gravity.

SIZING UP YOUR BACKPACK

For an accurate fit, your back should first be measured. Select a pack based on your torso length and try it on.

Measure from the prominent vertebrae at the base of the neck

Measure to the point in the small of the back level with the top of the hipbones

ADJUSTING THE FIT

Be sure that all parts of the pack fit comfortably with straps adjusted to allow for any changes in your weight or bulky clothing.

Shoulder straps should be snug but allow room for the arms to move freely

The sternum strap stabilizes the shoulder straps

Tightening the load lifters puts more weight on the shoulders

The hip belt should rest comfortably on your hipbones

PACKING YOUR BACKPACK

Keep your gear organized in waterproof stuff sacks to protect it from rain and keep it clean. Your daily essentials should be readily available, and the bulk of your heavy items should be as close to your back as possible in order to avoid the backpack pulling away from your shoulders. Lighter items should be toward the bottom of the pack.

ORGANIZING A BACKPACK

This is one of several ways to organize a backpack; every hiker takes slightly different gear and must fit it into a slightly different size and shape of pack.

Pack raingear and a waterproof sack containing extra layers, gloves, and a hat at the top of your pack where they are accessible

Put your first-aid kit where the contents are secure, and yet accessible

Place bags containing stove, eating utensils, and cook set close to the back, as they are heavy

Store food bags close to the back because they are likely to be heavy

Keep your clothing in a waterproof stuff sack to ensure that it stays dry

Secure your fuel bottle outside the pack in an upright position to minimize the risk of leakage

Tent poles are durable so can be strapped onto the bottom of your pack

Put your tent in a waterproof stuff sack and strap it to the outside of your pack

Use the bottom compartment of your pack for your sleeping mat and sleeping bag

Keep your sleeping bag in a waterproof stuff sack

Carry your water bottle where it is upright and accessible

Store daily essentials such as lip balm, snacks, sunglasses, a compass, a pocketknife, maps and guidebooks, insect repellent, and sunscreen in an outer pocket

Use a ditty (cloth) bag to hold personal essentials such as a roll of toilet paper

CARRYING SPARE PARTS

Packs are usually well made, but even the best construction cannot protect against a hiker who steps on a belt buckle or drops them down a rocky slope. A few simple items allow you to make necessary repairs:

■ Heavy-duty carpet needle and thread strong enough that you cannot break it with your hands
■ Extra belt buckle
■ Extra shoulder strap buckles
■ Clevis pins (for external-frame packs)
■ Pliers (for manipulating broken parts of external-frame packs)

WET WEATHER

Store items in protective bags in case of wet weather. Use the pouches of your pack to carry items you will need on a rainy day.
■ A top compartment is handy for items such as raingear, pack cover, and lunch.
■ A small pouch worn on your hip belt can be used to stow guidebook pages, a pocket knife, your compass, and insect repellent.
■ Be sure to protect electronic equipment in ziplocking bags or waterproof pouches.
■ A garbage bag is useful for waterproofing your sleeping bag or reinforcing your clothing bag stuff sacks.

Tents

Choosing your outdoor home is a matter of matching your needs to the many types of tents on the market. Look for the lightest tent available that meets your requirements. A two-person tent for temperate weather should weigh less than $5\frac{1}{2}$ lb (2.5 kg).

Tent construction

Three-season tents are designed for use in a variety of climates and have construction features found on most types of tents. The inner layer is made of lightweight material, which offers both insect protection and ventilation.

The flysheet and floor are made of waterproof fabric, which should extend about 4 in (10 cm) above the ground. Most tents use two or three poles, depending on whether they are built for low weight or stability.

THREE-SEASON TENT INNER
Typical of most tent designs, the three-season tent demonstrates how lightweight materials and innovative design features combine to give a secure, portable shelter.

Pole separates inner tent and flysheet, allowing air to circulate

Inner-tent material is uncoated to aid ventilation and disperse condensation

Swift clip
Securely attaches inner tent to poles quickly and easily

Panels of material allow tent to take an irregular shape

Seams are double-stitched to withstand tension

Pole sleeve
Guides pole around inner tent to distribute strain on sleeve evenly

Flysheet attachment
Color coded to allow each pole to be matched quickly to the right grommet

THREE-SEASON TENT WITH FLYSHEET

The flysheet extends in front of the tent to form a vestibule for gear storage, and provides good protection from the rain. When closed, an extended flysheet may result in poor ventilation.

Guy rope anchors tent securely against high winds

Outer door can be rolled horizontally and fixed to flysheet

Flysheet extends to the ground

Stash pocket
Mounted inside tent to provide space to stow gear that may be needed during the night

Stash door
Mounted on a smooth-running circular zipper. Door can be stowed in an internal stash pocket

Bathtub floor
Seam of tent floor is sewn above ground level, helping to prevent leakage during storms

Mesh door allows light in but prevents insects from entering

TENT FRAME DESIGN

Most tents use one of three basic frame designs. Innovative tent designs often incorporate elements from one or more of these basic shapes.

A-FRAME

The oldest design is the A-frame. Easy to pitch in poor weather, it does not suffer from condensation and is reasonably priced compared to tents using other frame designs.

Poles connect to form "A" shape

Steep pitch sheds water quickly

TUNNEL

The tunnel frame uses curved poles to achieve a greater internal volume than the A-frame, and tends to be less heavy.

Curved poles provide headroom

Only two poles means less weight

DOME

The dome frame also uses curved poles, but achieves greater rigidity by single or multiple crossings of the poles.

Rounded shape sheds snow

Poles cross for greater strength

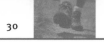
Choosing a tent

The secret to choosing the right tent is to have a clear idea of the terrain and weather you expect to be camping in. Tents are categorized according to the conditions they can be used in— a summer tent will be adequate for warm-weather trips, a three-season tent for both warm and cold conditions, and a winter tent for camping in severe weather.

CONSIDERING YOUR OPTIONS

Before buying a tent, consider the terrain and weather conditions in which the tent will be used, how many people it will need to sleep, and how much storage space it will take up. Also decide whether comfort or low weight is more important to you. If hiking with a partner, you can share the load of your tent, but if you plan to hike solo weight must be kept down.

SUMMER TENT

Sacrificing complete weather protection for views and ventilation, summer tents weigh less than three-season or winter tents. The inner tent is usually made of insect-proof netting, while the flysheet gives adequate coverage for warm-weather squalls, but may not withstand a mountain storm. Summer tents are best used in temperate climates below the treeline, since they are less stable in fierce storms than three-season and winter tents. Pitch them near sheltering trees or windbreaks.

Poles cross at a single point for light weight and stability

Dome shape offers good head room

Doors on either side allow easy entry and exit when sharing a tent

Flysheet does not reach the ground, giving good air circulation

Mesh fabric allows air to circulate

SUMMER TENT WITH FLYSHEET

SUMMER TENT WITHOUT FLYSHEET

THREE-SEASON TENT

The most versatile and popular tents available are three-season tents. They are suitable for use in a wide range of climates and terrain, including light snowfall and high mountains. Most versions have vestibule areas for gear storage, two or more poles for stability, and good flysheet coverage. Three-season tents can be either freestanding or secured with stakes; the latter are less convenient to pitch—especially when camping on rocky ground—but are lighter in weight.

Cam-lock clip attaches the inner tent to the poles for added security in poor weather

Mesh fabric and sealed-seam zip combine ventilation and waterproofing

Pockets mounted inside the tent provide space to stow gear

Flysheet extends all the way to the ground for good weather protection

Low rear of tent provides stability when it is pitched against the wind

Floor extends to give water protection

THREE-SEASON TENT WITH FLYSHEET

THREE-SEASON TENT WITHOUT FLYSHEET

WINTER TENT

In winter, heavy snowfall and high winds mean that safety as well as comfort are the primary factors in tent selection. For hiking in severe winter conditions, look for a tent that offers extra-strong poles, storm windows, and ample pockets for gear storage. The dome shape sheds snow well, and withstands high winds and heavy snow accumulation. But beware—these extra features can push the weight of a tent to more than 10 lb (4.5 kg). Choose the lightest tent with the features you need.

Fully enclosed pole sleeve provides extra stability in poor weather

Three criss-crossed poles provide excellent stability in strong winds and heavy snow

Condensation sponge absorbs moisture

Doorway allows hikers to cook in the vestibule without leaving their sleeping bags

Front vestibule provides space for gear storage

Zipper tag for easy opening

WINTER TENT WITH FLYSHEET

WINTER TENT WITHOUT FLYSHEET

ONE-PERSON TENT

A solo tent is heavier than a tarpaulin, but provides greater protection in extremely wet weather. Like bivvy shelters, they can be prone to condensation, and some of them have very limited headroom, making eating difficult when inside.

The front door can be rolled open for ventilation

Two hoop-style poles are part of the tent structure

BIVVY SHELTER

A bivvy shelter is smaller than a one-person tent. Bivvies usually consist of a single layer of waterproof, breathable fabric in the shape of a loose sleeping bag. While light to carry, they have little headroom and are prone to condensation.

Vestibule for storage

Limited height restricts you to a prone position

CARING FOR YOUR TENT

To ensure that your tent will continue to keep you warm and dry in cold, wet weather, you must take care of it:

■ Most manufacturers seal only the major seams of a tent, so you may need to seal minor ones with sealant glue.

■ Use a groundsheet under your tent to protect the fabric. This also prevents water from pooling beneath the tent.

■ Over time, tent fabric degrades with exposure to direct sunlight. Either take your tent down during the day or pitch it in a well-shaded area.

■ Clean your tent when you get home. Pitch it, hose it, and let it stand until it dries. It is best to do this in the evening, to reduce the tent's exposure to direct sunlight.

■ After many uses, tents may lose their water repellency. This can be restored with waterproofing treatment.

■ Store the dried tent in a stuff sack, or store it loose in a cool dry place.

Sleeping gear

After a hard day hiking, a good night's sleep is both appreciated and necessary. Choosing the right sleeping bag can help you to sleep comfortably—it should be warm enough for cold nights, yet not so warm that you are uncomfortably hot in milder conditions.

Sleeping bag features

A sleeping bag traps the air heated by your body and surrounds you with a protective shell of warm air. Fine filaments of down or synthetic fibers in the sleeping bag trap pockets of air, providing insulation. Thickly filled bags are the warmest, but quality and weight also need to be considered.

Cord lock
A locking mechanism secures the hood closed in cold weather, and can be loosened in mild weather

CHOOSING A SLEEPING BAG
When selecting a sleeping bag, you need to take into account its shape, insulating material, loft, construction methods, and individual features.

To retain body heat, a hood is essential for sleeping in colder weather. It should be roomy enough for you to turn your head

The sleeping bag should close securely around your shoulders, preventing warm air from escaping

Baffles are channels sewn into the bag to prevent the down from collecting in one area

Pocket
Some sleeping bags come equipped with accessory pockets, which can be used to store small items such as a key or wallet

Zipper
Ideally, a zipper should be snag resistant and have a draught tube—a thin strip of down that fits over the zipper on the inside of the bag, preventing heat from escaping and cold air from seeping in

SLEEPING BAG FILLINGS

Sleeping bags are made with either a down filling or a synthetic filling. Down sleeping bags are often used on high mountain expeditions because, for its weight, down is warmer than synthetic alternatives. It is also easier to compress, which is important when you have a lot of gear to fit into a small amount of space.

Goose down is better quality than duck down because it has more loft, which means that a goose down bag is warmer than a duck down bag of equivalent weight. Synthetic bags are preferable in damp climates because, unlike down, they retain some of their insulating value if they accidentally get wet. They also dry more quickly than down bags.

TEMPERATURE RATINGS

The warmth of a sleeping bag is identified by its temperature rating. In theory, a 32°F (0°C) bag should keep you warm in the stated temperature. If you are buying a three-season bag, look for the 32°F (0°C) rating. However, be aware that manufacturers differ in their standards, and hikers differ in their metabolisms, making temperature ratings an inexact science. Some manufacturers give a comfort rating and a survival rating, but these, too, are inexact.

In general, on a good quality bag, the fluffier the bag, the warmer it will be. In addition, the temperature rating can be affected by a number of design features, such as draught tubes on zippers and the shape of the hood. Where the top of the sleeping bag wraps around your shoulders is another important area— a snug fit here will stop warm air from seeping out.

DOWN FILLING

Down filling consists of very small, light, down feathers. The quality of down is measured according to fill and loft:
- Fill is another name for the down. It is rated according to its loft number (the volume). Known as the fill power rating, the loft is measured according to how much volume (in cubic inches) an ounce of fill takes up. Each manufacturer of down bags attaches a fill power rating to its insulation.
- The higher the loft number, the more efficient the insulation, so less filling is needed to fill a sleeping bag. This also means that the bag is lighter and more compact.

BAFFLES

Baffles are a feature of bag design that ensure an even spread of down.

SEWN-THROUGH

In this inexpensive construction, warm air may escape through uninsulated stitching.

BOXWALL

Mesh partitions at quilt lines prevent cold spots. It is costly, but very warm.

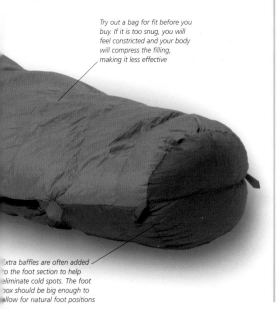

Try out a bag for fit before you buy. If it is too snug, you will feel constricted and your body will compress the filling, making it less effective

Extra baffles are often added to the foot section to help eliminate cold spots. The foot box should be big enough to allow for natural foot positions

Sleeping mats and accessories

In addition to a sleeping bag rated for the appropriate temperature, you will need a foam or air sleeping mat to ensure a comfortable and dry night's rest. Specialized gear, such as a mosquito net, a hammock, a space blanket, or an inflatable pillow may be needed in some environments.

SLEEPING MATS

An air or foam mat will not only help you to sleep more comfortably on hard or uneven ground, but will also provide insulation, preventing body heat from being lost through contact with the ground. The thicker the mat, the warmer it will be. Mats also act as a barrier between you and any moisture that may have seeped inside your tent.

AIR MATS

Available in different thicknesses, with some also containing a layer of foam, air mats provide superior comfort and thermal insulation. However, they are heavier and more expensive than foam mats. Self-inflating and blow-up mats are available, although most self-inflating mattresses do need extra inflation. Full-length mattresses are necessary in the winter. In the summer, a shorter length may suffice.

Some inflatable mats have a bumpy or textured surface that prevents you from slipping off

INFLATABLE MATS

FOLDED UP

FOAM MATS

The lightest and simplest type, foam mats simply roll up and may be strapped under a backpack. They are most comfortable when used on soft ground, such as sand or pine needles. Foam mats can also be used underneath an air mat for extra ground insulation in the winter.

Egg-crate surface traps pockets of warm air

FLAT FOAM MAT

ROLLED UP

Pitted, linear surface traps pockets of warm air

RIDGED FOAM MAT

PILLOW

An inflatable pillow is certainly not a necessity, but will add to your comfort. Alternatively, use a stuff sack filled with spare clothing or a rolled-up fleece top.

SLEEPING EASY

An inflatable pillow is an optional item—choose the lightest one available.

Rubberized cotton exterior can be wiped clean

Inflate according to comfort

SPACE BLANKET

A space blanket is made from lightweight heat-reflecting metallic material. It weighs less than an ounce, folds away easily, and gives emergency protection from poor weather.

QUICK WARM-UP
For maximum effect, wrap yourself up with the reflective side next to your body.

Aluminum coating reflects heat back to body

MOSQUITO NET

If you are sleeping under the stars, a mosquito net, which can be hung tarpaulinlike from a rope suspended between two trees, protects against insects.

Some are treated with insecticides

BUG PROTECTION
For comfort, mosquito nets provide protection from biting insects and allow air flow.

HAMMOCK

Carrying a hammock means that you can camp even if the ground is muddy, rocky, or inclined. With a hammock, anywhere with trees can be a campsite—a lightweight tarpaulin can be hung above you and staked to the ground in case of rain. Modern hammocks are designed to enable users to sleep in an almost flat position. If a hammock sags, lying diagonally flattens the hammock, giving more support to the spine.

HANGING A HAMMOCK
Position your hammock safely—somewhere with no dead tree branches above. Make sure the tree or upright is strong enough and that ropes are tied securely and will not slip.

Use an air mat for insulation and warmth, or a heat-reflecting pad. These can be ordered from some suppliers, or made by taping reflective metal foil to a foam mat

Secure the hammock tightly to the trees. The wide webbing on this hammock reduces damage to the bark

Cooking equipment

If hikers have anything in common, it is the appreciation of a good meal. Portable stoves and carefully chosen utensils make the cooking process quick and easy. Consider the complexity of the meals you want to cook, and the weight and bulk you are willing to carry.

Stoves

A portable stove allows you to cook anywhere you like without having to make a fire. Cooking over a stove is easier and safer than cooking over a fire, and is more environmentally friendly. Fires can cause unsightly scars on the landscape, especially in fragile environments such as arid regions and tundra. Your choice of stove may depend on what fuel is available.

ESTIMATING FUEL USE

Each type of stove requires a different amount of fuel, and each hiker has different cooking needs, so gauging fuel use is a matter of trial and error. Most stove manufacturers suggest how much fuel to take. Keep a record of what you cooked and how long your fuel lasted, to gauge your fuel consumption. A 11 fl oz (325 ml) bottle of fuel or a 6.7 oz (190 g) cylinder is usually more than adequate for a weekend hike. Make sure fuel bottles are free from leaks, as they will spoil food and damage other equipment.

FUEL AVAILABILITY

If hiking abroad, check with a local hiking organization or guidebook to find out which fuel is available locally. Fuel types most widely available may be paraffin, dry-cleaning fluid (which works in white gas stoves), and gas in cylinders.

HOW A LIQUID FUEL STOVE WORKS

Once primed—or pre-heated—a typical liquid fuel stove vaporizes fuel, mixes it with oxygen, and then burns it.

Fuel is preheated before entering the nozzle

Burner spreads flames evenly beneath pot

Priming cup heats the stove so fuel will combust

Fuel and air mixture exits stove

Foldable supports hold pots and pans

Fuel line must be kept clean

Fuel enters stove unit

Oxygen is introduced to fuel flow to aid combustion

Fuel bottle

Nozzle to control flow of fuel

Framework to hold and support the stove

Pump assembly for pressurizing fuel

STOVE COMPONENTS

Liquid fuel stoves usually have two main parts—a fuel bottle and a stove unit—connected by a fuel line.

Fuel line

Valve controls flow of fuel from bottle to stove

Stove unit

LIQUID FUEL STOVE

Most types of liquid fuel stove function on white gas, and may also be able to use unleaded gas, terpentine, and even dry cleaning fluid.

Large diameter fuel line for varied fuel types

Aluminum base reflects heat back to cooking pot

RELIABLE STOVE

Popular with mountaineering expeditions because of reliable performance, liquid fuel stoves perform well even in extreme cold and high altitudes.

CYLINDER STOVE

Easy to operate and lightweight, cylinder stoves use a blend of pressurized butane and propane. As the burners are small, these stoves are only suitable for use with small pots and pans.

Valve opens to allow gas to flow to burner

Use only small pots on small pot supports— oversize pots may topple over

Stove snaps or twists onto cylinder

SIMPLE STOVE

Although great when hiking in recreation-intensive areas where fuel is widely available, cylinder stoves do not perform well in very cold temperatures.

COMBINATION STOVE

While all combination stoves can use a variety of fuel types, such as white gas and unleaded gasoline, some models also take standard gas cylinders. Although heavy, these stoves are highly adaptable.

Fuel bottle can contain a variety of fuel types

Flame adjuster allows precise flame control

Burner suitable for windy conditions

VERSATILE STOVE

For trips when your fuel sources are uncertain, and if traveling to several different regions where fuel availability varies, choose a combination stove.

ALCOHOL STOVE

These are extremely lightweight and run on methylated spirits, which is sold in lightweight plastic bottles and is widely available in hardware stores.

Heat output is low so use a lid to conserve heat

Burner unit includes a simmering ring to regulate heat

LIGHTWEIGHT STOVE

If your meals require simple cooking, and if you are more concerned with saving weight than convenience, alcohol stoves are useful. Heat output is low, so boiling times are long.

QUESTIONS TO ASK BEFORE YOU BUY

Before you decide what type of stove to buy, ask yourself the following questions:
■ Are you looking for a lightweight stove?
■ Will you be cooking simple meals that require only a low heat output?

■ Are you hiking abroad and relying on the availability of local fuel?
■ Will your stove perform well if you are hiking in cold conditions or at high altitudes?
■ What size pots and pans will you be using?

Utensils and accessories

Successful cooking on the trail is a case of planning ahead, choosing your equipment, and being prepared to minimize. You can make a delicious meal with one small pot and a few simple ingredients—or you can pack a spice cabinet and a bevy of home-hydrated food for a gourmet feast.

ESSENTIAL COOKING ITEMS

Cooking gear should be lightweight. You will find multipurpose knives, utensils, dishes, food carriers, pots and pans sets, mugs, cups, and cleaning supplies at your local retailers. However, you should be able to use some of the supplies you have at home, if they are not too heavy.

MULTIPURPOSE KNIFE

In addition to a blade, a multipurpose knife should have a screwdriver, scissors, awl, can opener, wire cutters, and corkscrew. Its uses range from peeling carrots to whittling sticks. Look out for a miniature, lightweight model.

The corkscrew is an optional feature

A can opener is a useful feature for hikers

CUTLERY

A spoon usually suffices for most camping meals, although a combined spoon and fork is available, which does two jobs for the price and weight of one piece of cutlery. Choose utensils that are heatproof, lightweight, and robust.

A spoon is all most hikers need

A knife is optional if you are carrying a multipurpose knife

This fork doubles as a can opener

DISHES

A plastic bowl meets almost all outdoor eating needs. Choose one that fits inside your cooking pot to save space. If hiking with a partner, choose nesting bowls (one bowl fits inside the other) to save even more space.

FOOD CARRIERS

The best way to carry food is in a nylon stuff sack. Count out precise portions of the major ingredients for each meal, discard removable packaging, and pack the food into plastic ziplock bags. Staples such as dried milk, sugar, and spices can also be stored in these bags, although small quantities of spices can be kept in miniature plastic containers.

A waterproof sack is a good choice. Hang it from a tree to keep your food safe from animals

Buy small containers for storing spices, but do not carry too many as they add weight and take up space

QUESTIONS TO ASK BEFORE YOU BUY

Before you choose your equipment, ask yourself the following questions:

■ How much storage space do you have?
■ What kind of meals will you be cooking and what do you need to prepare them?
■ How many people will you be cooking for?
■ Is there anything on your list that you can do without—for example, a frying pan?
■ Can you share any of the equipment with hiking partners to avoid doubling up?

POTS AND PANS SETS

A set of nesting pots that stack inside each other is a popular choice, but there is a danger of taking more pots than you actually need. Assess your cooking requirements, and if possible, take just one pot. Always take the lid—it saves fuel and cuts down on the cooking time. Aluminum pans are a good choice because they heat quickly—but they can burn food if not attended. Titanium pots are expensive, but are extremely durable and light.

Clip is designed to be used with a pot-grabber, which hooks on to the clip and becomes a handle

Rounded edges encourage even heat distribution up the sides

Tight-fitting lid makes cooking quicker and more economical

Lids with flat tops can also double up as plates or shallow bowls

A pot-grabber can be attached to the pan, making it safer to pick up when hot

A large pot is a good choice if you will be cooking for more than one person

MUGS AND CUPS

Insulated mugs keep soups and drinks hot in cold weather. Nesting cups made of Lexan® are tough and heatproof, yet light and easy to pack. Avoid using enamel or metal mugs, which are often the cause of burned lips.

Lid to keep in warmth

LIFEVENTURE

Insulation keeps drinks and soups hot

Lightweight plastic is inexpensive and does not break

CLEANING SUPPLIES

A scouring-pad will keep your pot and eating utensils clean. A synthetic pad will last longer than a sponge and does not retain odors. Use a few drops of multiuse liquid soap (carried in a small plastic bottle) for washing dishes.

Metal scouring-pad for pots used on a fire

Synthetic pads for dishes and pots used on a stove

Essential equipment

A clean supply of water is essential on a hike, and carrying enough
fresh water or being able to treat supplies is a requirement. A first-aid
kit is also invaluable, while a flashlight, a watch, a hygiene kit, a map
case, and an air mat repair kit are all worth finding space for.

Water carriers

Carrying water for a short day hike
is usually no problem—you need only
a lightweight water bottle with a tight
lid. Most packs have external pockets
to slot a bottle into, or attach it to
your pack or belt with a loop-top lid.
To stay hydrated on the move, a sport
bottle top makes drinking easier, or
choose a hydration system. For camp,
a water carrier bag can be packed.

WATER BOTTLES
For a longer hike, choose a durable
bottle. Nalgene™ polycarbonate bottles
can withstand freezing cold or boiling
hot liquids. Aluminum bottles are
lightweight and virtually unbreakable.

MAKING A PRACTICAL CHOICE
A bottle with a wide mouth means you can more
easily scoop water from a shallow source. A
narrow-necked bottle is easier to drink from.

WATER CARRIER BAG
Large bags are convenient for long
waterless stretches and for carrying
water from a water source to a campsite.
Small bags are useful as they can be
balanced in different parts of your pack.

CARRYING WATER
These water carrying bags weigh very little when
empty, but can carry up to several pints of water.
Each pint of water weighs $2^{1}/_{2}$ lb (1 kg).

Bag folds neatly
away when not
carrying water

Opening for
filling combined
with tap for easy
pouring

HYDRATION SYSTEMS
Consisting of a lightweight plastic
bladder and drinking tube, these are
built into a pack. Alternatively, they can
be bought separately and put inside your
daypack or waist pack. The tube
allows you to take a drink of water
effortlessly while on the move,
making it easier to stay hydrated.

HYDRATION PACK
An integrated water carrier is built
into the pack. Water is sipped through
a tube that passes over the shoulder.

Drink tube with
bite-valve

Durable plastic
bladder carries 4 pints
(1.8 liters) water

HYDRATION BAG

Equipment for treating water

If you have to find drinking water in the wild, it is always best to treat it. Microorganisms that can cause intestinal problems may be present, caused by contamination by wildlife, farm animals, pollutants, or other hikers. Spring water taken directly from the source in high mountain wildernesses may be uncontaminated, but to be safe, treat all drinking water.

SAUCEPAN

The most basic way to kill parasites is to bring water to a rolling boil for at least a minute—the only gear required is a pan and a stove. This works well when treating cooking water and water for hot drinks, but it is not practical for refilling water bottles during a hike.

CHEMICAL TREATMENT TABLETS

Iodine tablets will enable you to clean water in a container such as your water bottle, without the need for any extra equipment. Simply add the tablets to your water, then leave for up to 20 minutes (see p.107). Additional tablets are available to counteract the distinctive taste of iodine. Alternatively, keep some lemon peel in your water bottle.

FILTER

To strain out most parasites and microorganisms, you can use a ceramic or charcoal based filter. It will not, however, remove viruses (which are common in less-developed countries).

COMBINED FILTER AND TREATMENT

These units contain an iodine element, which kills viruses, as well as a filtering system, which strains out parasites and microorganisms. Some units are modified water bottles—water passes through a filtering and treatment system before emerging clean from the spout.

Handle is pulled up to draw up the piston

Handle is pushed down to press down the piston

Water exits the ceramic filters and is forced from the outlet

As the piston is pulled up, the vacuum created draws in water

Porous ceramic filter

Piston

Water is forced through the holes into the ceramic filters

Water is taken in through the open valve

The valve is closed so that the water cannot escape

THE WATER FILTER

Water is drawn in when the handle pulls the piston upward. When the piston is pushed downward, the water is forced through the ceramic filter.

CARING FOR YOUR FILTER

■ Filters clog when contaminants build up in the filter. If using one with a replaceable cartridge, always carry a spare. Cartridges can sometimes be cleaned in the field.
■ Follow the manufacturer's directions for cleaning whenever your filter becomes sluggish or difficult to operate.

■ Some filters can be scrubbed clean with a brush. Others can be backwashed, by which contaminants are removed by running clean water and bleach back through the filter element, which is then rinsed thoroughly.
■ To prolong a filter's working life, use a pre-filter to strain out the largest contaminants.

First-aid kit

Like a spare tire, a first-aid kit is something you hope you will never have to use. Both items share another quality—they need to be checked regularly. Adhesives can deteriorate in humid conditions, so replace items like bandages every few trips. Also, check use-by dates on medication.

KIT CONTENTS

Commercially available first-aid kits are useful, but the contents need to be tailored for a wilderness setting and the length of your hike. You may need to add more pain killers, and some items that are not commonly included, such as itch relief for insect bites. Specially designed kits for hikers are available at outdoor retailers.

Scissors, which may be on a multipurpose knife, are essential for cutting tape and trimming nails

Micropore or zinc oxide tape is useful for holding dressings in place

Crepe bandage is used to support muscle or joint injuries, secure dressings, or to apply pressure to control bleeding

Antiseptic cleaning swabs (not visible) are essential for cleaning wounds—and your hands

A disposable syringe can be used to irrigate a wound

Sterile wound dressings are used to cover bleeding wounds

Adhesive strips are perfect for covering small cuts, and are also useful for holding bandages in place

Conforming gauze bandages stretch, so are ideal for joint support where some mobility is still required

Pain killers, such as aspirin, should be saved for emergencies

Hypodermic needles are especially useful when traveling in developing countries—if you need an injection, a clean needle protects against infections

LIFESYSTEMS™

FIRST-AID KIT
Pack a small flashlight in your first-aid kit to ensure that you can find what you need in the dark.

CARRYING ADDITIONAL MEDICAL SUPPLIES

Remember to take any personal medications, including any that you use only infrequently but might need while on your hike. Take copies of doctor's prescriptions that you may need to replenish during your trip. You should also take:

■ Malaria tablets if you are traveling in a region of the world where it is prevalent.

■ Plastic face shield or pocket mask to protect you and a casualty from infections when giving rescue breaths.
■ Survival bag to provide immediate warmth in almost any emergency.
■ Treatment for rashes and insect bites including sprays, antihistamine pills, and anti-inflammatory ointments to stop itching.

Useful extras

The items required for a trip will usually differ from person to person. Over time, develop a list of items you generally find useful (and jettison items that you find you never need). Your list will also change depending on the climate, the terrain, the length of trip, and the likelihood of finding supplies en route.

ITEMS TO CONSIDER

Good personal hygiene can help prevent minor cuts from becoming infected, so you may want to take biodegradable soap in a container. Multipurpose items are very useful—a watch can double up as an alarm clock or a barometer. Ziplock bags are ideal for protecting items from damp, dust, and insects, and for organizing items in your pack.

HYGIENE KIT

Personal requirements will vary, but a basic kit could contain a small travel comb, a razor, a small tube of toothpaste, and a travel toothbrush. You may also need a small amount of biodegradable soap measured into a plastic container.

Disposable razor with extra blades

Traveler's toothbrush, with detachable case for brush head

Sample-size toothpaste

Lightweight 3-in (75-mm) comb

WATCH

Choose a watch with an alarm. Some watches also have features such as a compass, barometer, and altimeter, which can help you monitor your progress and location.

Water-resistant case with a large-digit, back-lit display

AIR MAT REPAIR KIT

If you have an air mat, a repair kit is essential in case of punctures. It can also be used to patch other items, such as raingear, tents, and sleeping bags.

Air mat repair kit includes patches and glue

ZIPLOCK BAGS

You can protect everything from clothing to matches, and food to electronic equipment, with a ziplock bag. The zip seals tightly while allowing the contents to stay flat. The fastenings are not very robust, so take spare bags.

WATERPROOF MAP CASE

A see-through waterproof map case enables you to navigate even in bad weather without worrying about ruining your maps.

A rolldown Velcro® closure keeps out the water

Clear plastic case means your map stays visible

Toggle allows you to adjust length of neck cord

Specialist equipment

Sticks and trekking poles can make the going easier, while animal-proof bags and containers will protect your equipment from hungry or inquisitive creatures. You may also want to take a camera, GPS, or binoculars to enhance your enjoyment of the hiking experience.

Trekking poles and hiking sticks

Poles and sticks can help to prevent the aches and pains that affect many hikers, especially any who are older or overweight, or who have injury-prone knees. Walking poles reduce the pressure on the back, legs, and especially the knees, by transferring weight onto the arms. A single pole can be used, but for the optimum level of support, many hikers prefer two.

TYPES OF POLES AND STICKS

Features to look for are graphite tips for better traction, spring-loaded shock absorbers to take pressure off the knees and absorb the shock of a steep step or hop downhill, and ergonomically angled cork hand grips. These will absorb sweat so the hands do not develop blisters.

Traditional walking stick

Ski poles
Flick-lock is a quick and secure mechanism for adjusting the length of your pole

A strap stops you from dropping the pole

Slanted grips are ergonomically designed

Very strong, light shaft that can flex without damage

Antishock spring system provides cushioning (inside shaft)

Basket
A basket stops the pole from sinking into the surface, such as snow or mud

Telescoping poles
Measurements help you to keep track of your preferred length of pole

Very strong shaft, usually made of titanium or aluminum

125 cm
120 cm
115 cm

WALKING STICK

SKI POLE

Different tips are used for different surfaces

Nonslip tips
Graphite tips keep poles from slipping on wet rock

TREKKING POLES

ALTERNATIVE USES FOR POLES

- Warding off aggressive animals
- Providimg strong tarpaulin support
- Providimg a stable, monopod support for a camera (though not all poles are suitable)

Animal-proof equipment

Sometimes wild animals become so used to humans that they begin to visit campsites, often with the intention of begging for or stealing food. This is a problem not only for you but also for the animals, who can grow dependent on an unnatural diet. When hiking in popular recreational areas, always take the necessary equipment to guard your food from animals.

TAKING PRECAUTIONS AT CAMP

The usual method of keeping food away from animals is to hang it in a tree (*see* p.131). However, in certain regions, bears and other animals have become skilled at finding food in trees, which necessitates using alternative strategies, such as bear-proof canisters, bear-proof stuff sacks, and hanging food from poles with ropes.

BEAR-PROOF CONTAINERS

Bear-proof canisters are hard plastic carriers for food. In some parks, they can be rented, and typically hold about five days' worth of food. Bear-proof stuff sacks made of the same fabric used in bullet-proof vests are also effective. For attaching food to ropes on poles, a karabiner (metal clip used in mountaineering) is useful.

KEEPING FOOD AWAY FROM ANIMALS

Choose a tree that is well away from your sleeping area and a branch that is strong enough to hold your stores. Suspend the food at least 12 ft (3.5 m) above the ground and well away from the trunk.

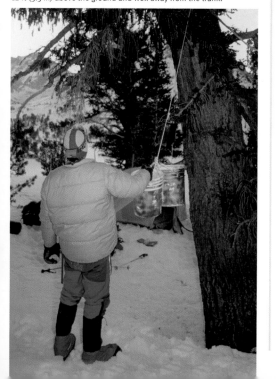

RODENT-PROOFING

Bears are not the only animals that steal your food. Mice and rats are often found in popular campsites, hiking shelters, and huts. A contraption that keeps rodents from your stores can be easily made on site. You will need a pocketknife, a tin can, 3 ft (90 cm) of cord or rope, and a small stick.

Nail / Tin can
Cord / Stick
Knot / Canvas bag

1 Use the pocketknife to puncture a hole in the base of an empty food can.
2 Hold the can upside down and thread a short piece of cord through the hole. Tie a knot in the rope underneath the can to hold it in place, leaving about a 1 ft (30 cm) length of rope under the knot.
3 Tie the upper part of the rope to the nail. Tie a stick to the bottom of the rope in a perpendicular position.
4 Hang your food from the stick. The mice cannot get past the can to the food.

Tools and gadgets

You do not need to load up your pack with every gadget and electronic tool that has been invented for outdoor enthusiasts. But many of these items have functions that are useful in extreme weather or difficult terrain. Make sure the ones you choose are good quality and will not let you down.

ALTIMETER

When navigating in mountainous terrain it is useful to have an altimeter. By using changes in atmospheric pressure, it measures your elevation above sea level.

LOCATING YOUR POSITION

If properly adjusted to the correct elevation at your starting-point, you can use an altimeter, along with a map, to determine your location.

Easy-to-read display face gives accurate readings up to 29,500 feet (9,000 m)

Function buttons can be operated with gloves on

PEDOMETER

It is always interesting to record how far you have walked, and a pedometer provides this information. Knowing this distance can also help you navigate.

INDICATING DISTANCE

Most pedometers count your footsteps, then calculate distance. To be accurate, you must first measure the length of your stride.

Digital display shows the distance and number of steps

Set your weight and stride length to begin

CELL PHONE

When hiking solo, especially in remote areas, a cell phone is useful in case you need to call for help. However, there may be no signal, and nowhere to recharge the battery, so it is no substitute for good judgement; or an excuse to take risks.

KEEPING IN TOUCH

Be discreet when using your cell phone in popular wilderness areas—other hikers may not want to hear your conversations.

Most cell phones double up as clocks

A sturdily constructed phone is more hardwearing on the trail

BINOCULARS

Although most often used for spotting wildlife and birds, or to take a closer look at features or landmarks in the distance, binoculars are also a useful navigation aid when looking for the path, or searching for a viable cross-country route.

GETTING A GOOD VIEW

From ornithology to astronomy, a rugged but lightweight pair of binoculars will enhance your enjoyment of the natural world.

Look for solid construction of the focus adjustment

Larger lenses gather more light to give a clear and detailed view

GPS

The Global Positioning System (GPS) uses multiple signals from satellites to determine your position on earth. GPS is extremely accurate—you can fix your position to within 10 ft (3 m).

Systems designed for backpackers sometimes include footpath data. You can input your own information to help you find a path or a route, or to recall a route later. GPSs can also calculate approximate travel time.

MILITARY MUSCLE

Originally developed for military use, the cost of commercial GPS systems has fallen to make them more affordable.

Graphic shows use of satellites to plot position

READY
TO NAVIGATE

SPEED
0.0ᵐ

NAVIGATION SCREEN

Bearing arrow will appear here

READY
TO NAVIGATE
ACCURACY:
18ft

SIGNAL

Walking speed

COMPASS SCREEN

Operation buttons on side of unit

Menu screen allows the user to scroll through the unit's features

MENU

MARK

WAYPOINTS

ROUTE

TRACKS

SETUP

18:01:07

Compass arrow shows north

Animated figure "walks" with you

ME

500mi

MAP SCREEN

ALL MAPPED OUT

Simple GPS systems are used as a navigational aid in conjunction with a map (*see* p.81).

BEFORE YOU BUY

Before you decide what type of GPS to look for, consider the following questions:
■ Do you want a simple model, to be used with a traditional map, or one with map storage and download facilities?
■ Do you want to know your altitude as well as your position? If so, choose a model with an onboard barometric altimeter.
■ Is the size and weight a concern? Simpler units are often smaller and lighter.
■ Do you require other features, such as night sky information, waterproof casing, a calendar, or enhanced battery life?

Photography

Taking photographs is an excellent way to record the places you have visited on hiking trips. But if you want to bring home high-quality pictures, you face special challenges. First, weight limitations restrict the amount of equipment you can carry. And second, the rigors of being outdoors in all weather can be harmful to delicate photographic equipment and film.

DIGITAL CAMERA

A digital camera is an excellent choice because it allows you to take several shots, review them, and choose the one you like best—something that is important when shooting action pictures or wildlife, where you cannot control the photographic subject. Some digital cameras are small enough to fit in the palm of your hand (a bonus for weight-conscious hikers), but they must be carefully protected against rain and dirt. On a long trip, unless you have a laptop with you on to which you can upload images from the camera, you will need to carry additional memory cards.

FILM-FREE
The popularity of digital cameras has grown along with their picture quality and affordability.

Function dial
Manual selection of functions including automatic setting

Viewfinder
The image can be framed through the viewfinder and on a small LCD screen

Flash
Autoflash function can be turned on and off manually

AF/self-timer light
Helps camera to focus automatically, and to take time-delayed shots

Lens
Automatic zoom lens with 3x optical zoom on standard model

POINT-AND-SHOOT CAMERA

Point-and-shoot cameras are available in both digital and standard film formats. Some companies make point-and-shoot weatherproof models that are as lightweight as standard versions, but can be used in wet weather and even be immersed in water up to a depth of 10 ft (3 m) or more. They allow you to take shots in challenging conditions.

MAKE IT SNAPPY
Compact, lightweight, and easy to use, a point-and-shoot camera has much to commend it to the hiker. These cameras run on batteries, so pack extras.

Shutter
Squeeze gently to take the shot

Lens
Automatic zoom lens with 3x optical zoom

Flash
Automatic function for shots taken in poor light

Viewfinder
The image is seen through a separate viewfinder lens

SINGLE LENS REFLEX CAMERA

A traditional single lens reflex (SLR) camera uses 35-mm film and has interchangeable lenses. These cameras, which can produce excellent results, are best for serious photographers, but may be too complex and heavy for the needs of most hikers.

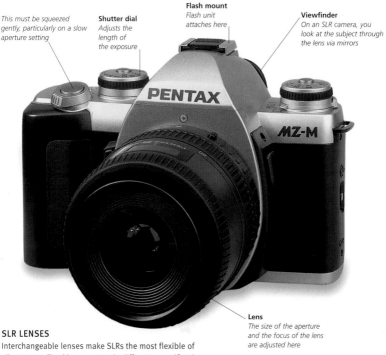

This must be squeezed gently, particularly on a slow aperture setting

Shutter dial
Adjusts the length of the exposure

Flash mount
Flash unit attaches here

Viewfinder
On an SLR camera, you look at the subject through the lens via mirrors

Lens
The size of the aperture and the focus of the lens are adjusted here

SLR LENSES

Interchangeable lenses make SLRs the most flexible of all cameras. Fixed lenses come in different magnifications, wide-angle lenses increase the angle of view, and telephoto zoom lenses are excellent for both distant or close-up shots. Colored filters can be added for effect.

FILM AND LENSES FOR AN SLR

FILM

■ Choose film for the light conditions you expect to encounter. Most outdoor photographers shoot ASA 60–100 in bright sun. In shadier areas, ASA 200 may give you more flexibility.
■ In warm climates, store film right in the center of your pack, perhaps insulated in a bag full of clothing. In subfreezing weather, handle film slowly and gently, because it can crack and tear.
■ Film can pass safely through airport X-ray machines if it is lower than ASA 800 and if you do not go through many checkpoints. Alternatively, you can ask to have your film hand-inspected. To avoid X-ray machines, you can have your film developed or you can send it home by mail.

LENSES

■ Limit yourself to two or three lenses if possible, or it will significantly increase pack weight.
■ Choose suitable lenses for the type of pictures you wish to take—portraits, panoramic scenery, wildlife, or indoors with subdued lighting work well with different types of lenses.
■ Using a zoom lens allows you to magnify the subject, offering great flexibility for hikers at a reasonable weight. Telephoto lenses are heavy and often require the use of a tripod.
■ A lens hood is an umbrella for your lens—it shades the lens from too much sunlight.

ORGANIZING
A HIKE

Organizing a local hike

Local day or overnight hikes offer a wonderful opportunity to test your hiking legs, become familiar with your gear, and learn new skills. Hiking close to home reduces travel time, allows you to experiment in a familiar environment, and reschedule easily if the weather turns bad.

Planning a day hike

A day hike can be anything you want it to be, from a gentle foray near your home to a challenging hike further afield. It also provides a chance to prepare yourself for a longer hike—you can try out new gear, increase your level of fitness, and discover how far you can walk comfortably in a day.

DECIDING WHERE TO GO

Look in outdoor stores for local guidebooks, or ask the staff for their recommendations. Many large parks have extensive trail systems and publish their own maps and trail guides, which will describe the level of difficulty of a hike. If none are available, gauge the difficulty by talking to park guides or other walkers. It is vital to understand how to read the landscape on a map before setting out. What starts as a gentle stroll in the hills can become quite strenuous further along the route, and may even involve a perilous rock climb.

When calculating how long a hike will take, it is important to know how much ground you can cover comfortably in an hour, and for how many hours you can walk. Many people overestimate their fitness. Unless you are used to walking all day, your pace is likely to slow considerably toward the end of the hike.

Try several short local hikes before you make a full-day hike. If you are hiking in a group, base your pace on the ability of the slowest member. Once you know your average walking pace, use the table below as a guide to judge how far, and at what speed, you can walk in a day.

GAUGING SPEED AND DISTANCE

INTENSITY OF HIKE	AVERAGE SPEED	RECOMMENDED LENGTH OF DAY HIKE
Leisurely	2 mph (3 km/h)	3–5 miles (4.5–8 km)
Moderate	2½ mph (4 km/h)	4–6 miles (6.5–9.5 km)
Strenuous	3 mph (5 km/h)	6 miles and over (9.5 km and over)

Add 30 minutes for every 1,000 ft (300 m) of elevation gain. Also allow about 10 minutes' rest time per hour of hiking.

POINT OF INTEREST

An interesting feature, such as a waterfall, makes an ideal halfway point to your hike. Ensure you are wearing adequate footwear for the conditions.

CHOOSING A ROUTE

There are several types of route from which to choose. A loop hike is a circular walk in which you return to the start without retracing your steps. Sometimes you can make a loop by stringing together segments of several different trails. If you cannot find a loop hike, you might take a there-and-back hike by walking to an interesting destination, then retracing your steps. Alternatively, if you have hiking partners and two cars, you can shuttle cars to each end of the trail, then take a one-way hike from one end to the other, to avoid incurring any transportation problems.

ASSESSING THE AREA

Most areas offer several types of hike, such as the one-way and loop hikes shown below. Check your map for key features such as tricky terrain, water sources, and parking facilities.

N
W   E
S

1 KM

1 MILE

Parking site at end of one-way hike

Woodland gives shelter from the sun in hot weather

Waterfall provides a point of interest to hike around

River provides water for filtering and drinking

Trail passes scenic mountainous area

Steep incline

Start and finish point for loop hike

KEY

—— One-way hike

—— Loop hike

 Parking lot

Wooded area

Rocky terrain

Water feature

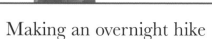

Making an overnight hike

For your first overnight hike, choose a nearby destination when the weather forecast is good. By sticking to easy terrain in gentle countryside, you will have the chance to pace yourself and learn the basic techniques of camping and cooking without having to cope with unfamiliar conditions.

CHOOSING A TRAIL

A hiking guidebook to your region will probably have dozens of suggestions for trails. Look for well-marked, easy trails with established campsites and adequate sources of water. When you have narrowed your selection down to a few trails, ask members of a local hiking club, a salesperson at an outdoor store, or the organization that manages the land for their recommendations.

PLANNING FOR COMFORT AND SAFETY

Perhaps the most common mistake made by newcomers to overnight hiking is planning too ambitiously. Walking along a trail is very different from walking in a town. The constantly shifting pressure of uneven ground affects muscles very differently from the pressure of sidewalks, where each step is the same. Also, the added weight of a backpack increases the effort needed to take each step. New hikers are often surprised by sore muscles and blisters. For these reasons, it is better to plan a short hike than to attempt a long and difficult trail on your first time out.

Safety issues should be a factor in your planning. Avoid camping above the treeline, especially in passes or on ridges, where you might be exposed to storms. If there are river fords, be sure to check on water levels before your hike. In spring, many hiking trails may retain snow or ice, or may be muddy or boggy. In arid areas, find out whether seasonal water sources are likely to be running or dry. The more information you gather about conditions beforehand, the more enjoyable your hike is likely to be.

SETTING UP CAMP

Plan to arrive at your camping destination well before nightfall, so that you have time to put up your tent and prepare your meal in daylight.

Allow sufficient time to prepare sleeping arrangements before nightfall

In order to put up your tent quickly and easily, practice erecting it before your first hike

HIKING WITH OTHERS

An overnight hike is a wonderful way to share uninterrupted time with family and friends. Another person's perspective and judgement also adds an element of safety to a hike. Several people can share the weight of gear such as tents and cooking equipment.

MAPPING A ROUTE

This circular hiking route has varied scenery and terrain, and a refuge point. It covers a total distance of about 12 miles (20 km), divided between two days.

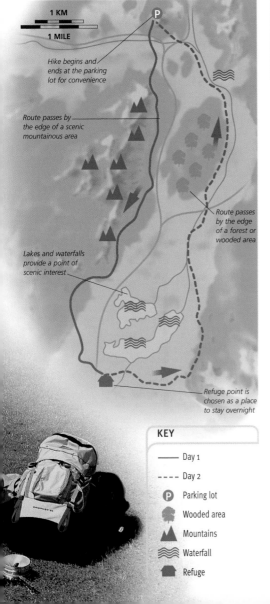

Hike begins and ends at the parking lot for convenience

Route passes by the edge of a scenic mountainous area

Route passes by the edge of a forest or wooded area

Lakes and waterfalls provide a point of scenic interest

Refuge point is chosen as a place to stay overnight

KEY

——— Day 1

- - - Day 2

P Parking lot

Wooded area

Mountains

Waterfall

Refuge

PLANNING YOUR ROUTE

A detailed itinerary is not usually required for a simple overnight hike, although if permits are required, you may need to commit to a campsite in advance. Generally, you should decide how much distance you want to cover: 6–8 miles (10–13 km) a day is generally far enough for beginners; fit hikers can easily double that. Check the guidebook to be sure there are campsites or refuges at the distances you want to cover. Also check for water sources and whether there are any long climbs that will slow you down.

ESTIMATING DISTANCE

If you are planning an easy, conservative distance, you should have no problem making it to your campsite before dark. But if you have only half a day to hike, or are planning to cover a long distance, make sure you have enough time. Always take account of the weight of your pack, any climbs, difficult terrain, and the fitness of your companions when estimating your distance. Also factor in time for resting, eating, and stretching (*see* pp.70–3).

PERMITS AND REGULATIONS

Many parks, forests, and reserves regulate camping. In some regions, permits are required, reservations may be recommended, or you may have to use designated campsites each time you set up camp.

Organizing an independent trip

A hiking trip lasting several days or more will necessitate greater research and planning, and you will need to think carefully about the equipment and food you take with you. If you are hiking abroad, you may also need to organize visas and travel insurance.

Researching your destination

A hike that lasts a few days or more is a chance for a real break from your everyday routine. Such a trip will involve taking time off work and incur travel and equipment expenses, so it is important that you find an interesting trail and visit it at the right time of year. Research trail conditions, traveling to the trail (which may require visas), and any health issues.

CHOOSING A TRAIL

Once you have decided on a destination and the kind of hike you want to undertake, you can get a sense of the wide variety of hiking experiences by attending meetings at local hiking clubs, where members often give slide shows about recent trips. More experienced friends and staff at local outdoor leisure stores may be able to recommend trails. You can also find information in hiking or camping magazines. If you have decided on a particular park or reserve, call the management office to ask about their recommendations for hikes that meet your criteria. For your first few trips, look for relatively well-known trails rather than trying to devise your own routes in remote areas.

INTERNET RESEARCH

The internet is an ever-expanding source of useful information about hiking destinations. Type in the address of a recommended website or use one of the search engines to find general or specific information about a hiking location and possible trails.

USING MAPS AND GUIDEBOOKS

Try to find up-to-date material. It is worth getting in touch with land managers before you go, to check that trails described in guidebooks are open.

Local maps can be purchased when you reach the local area

A map is an essential tool, especially when hiking independently

Books can provide invaluable detail

INTERNET HELP

Finding the right website is a useful tool in planning a hike. It can give advice, suggest routes, and help you buy books online.

Browse the site to plan your trip

Hiking World

Trail Conservation & Policy | Events & Volunteer Opportunities | News & Resources | Hiker's Store | Guest Book | Site Map

Browse by Map | Search by Keyword | National Parks

FIND A TRAIL
FIND A MAP
FIND A GUIDEBOOK
ACCOUNT
SHOPPING CART

Trail Finder   USA

Search by Keyword
Enter Keyword(s):

Select Region:
Search All
Search

MEXICO:
CARIBBEAN:
CANADA:
Alberta | British Columbia | Manitoba | New Brunswick | Newfoundland | Northwest Territories | Nova Scotia | Ontario | Prince Edward Island | Quebec | Saskatchewan | Yukon

Select a region to research | *Choose an area for trail info or a route map* | *Click on a link to go to other useful sites*

CHOOSING GUIDEBOOKS

Libraries, bookstores, outdoor gear stores, and internet booksellers are all good sources of guidebooks. If you are traveling far from home, some internet research may yield information about guidebooks that may not be readily available in your home country. In addition to describing the actual route a trail takes, guidebooks usually provide information about nearby lodgings, campsites, water sources, trail difficulties and challenges, access to the start, local transportation, seasonal conditions, and a host of other issues.

CHOOSING MAPS

Hiking maps can be very difficult to find, especially if your destination is far away. Most hiking guidebooks contain at least rudimentary maps, but these may not have the detailed topographical information that you need for navigating (*see* pp.76–7). Guidebooks usually note which maps are recommended for a hike and the contact information for buying them. Failing this, you should be able to find them in stores at or near your destination.

FINDING YOUR WAY

Having the right map, a guidebook that describes the route, and a compass, will help you to follow your chosen trail on an independent hike.

INTERNET SEARCHES

The internet can give you a great deal of information, but you need to choose your sites with care.

■ Outdoor-related sites provide useful information on all aspects of hiking. They often have chat rooms where you can compare notes with other hikers.

■ The individual websites of other hikers may give you reports and information about particular trails. However, you have no way of knowing if they have come from an experienced mountaineer or a hiking newcomer. You may be able to email the author to request further information.

■ Sites may help you find relevant guidebooks or offer pages on a pay-per-download basis. The guarantee of professionally produced material may be well worth the fee.

■ *See* pp.150–2 for selected web links.

Making travel plans

Perhaps more than any other kind of travel, a hiking trip reflects the personality of the traveler. While some trips are flexible, others are carefully planned down to the smallest detail. But whatever your style, do consider transportation to and from the trail, as well as your food and shelter.

PLANNING AHEAD

Most independent backpacking trips require less planning than a traditional vacation, because you do not have to rent a property, make hotel reservations, or organize your daily transportation. (Your tent is your accommodation and your feet are your means of travel.) But on some trips, you may have to make reservations for campsites or refuges, and on longer hikes, you may want to arrange for food supplies to be mailed to various locations at intervals along your route. In addition, you will need to consider transportation logistics, such as how you will travel to and from the start of the trail.

OPEN-AIR MEETING POINT

Hikers meet at a cairn on a trail in the Scottish Highlands. Sharing the experience with others is one of the great pleasures of hiking.

BOOKING YOUR TRIP

Unless you are driving to your chosen destination, you will need to arrange air, train, or boat travel. These matters are simple to book on the Internet or by phone. For information on the trail itself, including details of guided trips, contact small, locally owned operators based in your destination. These are likely to be more helpful than your own local travel agent, who will probably be unfamiliar with areas away from tourist destinations, and may not have contacts in, or experience of, the remote regions often frequented by hikers.

HIKING SOLO OR IN COMPANY

Most hiking authorities recommend that you hike with a partner or in a group, because this adds an element of security in the case of accident or emergency. It is also very sensible and practical because you can share the weight of communal gear such as tents and cooking equipment. Hiking in company also allows you to share your experiences.

CONVIVIAL REFUGE
Mountain huts offer refuge in bad weather, as well as a place to meet and socialize with fellow travelers. Hut staff are usually hospitable and can be an invaluable source of local information.

Some hikers on popular trails set off alone, but are happy to join up with compatible fellow hikers. This strategy works best when you are hiking in places with well-developed trekking routes, or if you are following a route with well-established "stages" where people stop to eat, sleep, and socialize.

ARRANGING FOOD SUPPLIES

You may be able to send boxes of food on ahead to be held for you at hotels where you will be a guest, or at post offices. Alternatively, you can buy food in towns and villages en route—although it may be heavy to carry, unfamiliar, too easily perishable, or otherwise not ideal for hiking.

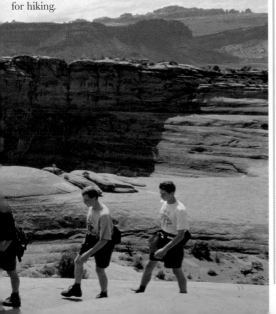

BUDGETING

Hiking trips are generally inexpensive, especially if you do not have the cost of hotels and restaurants.
- Start by determining how much you can afford to spend and set a budget.
- Remember to allow extra money for travel to and from the start of the trail, if necessary.
- Guidebooks will provide information about the costs of campgrounds, refuges, or inns.
- Allow enough money to treat yourself to the occasional restaurant meal.
- Food costs vary according to the region but are almost never more expensive than eating at home.
- On long hikes, keep an emergency budget reserve for replacing broken gear, as well as consumables such as film, insect repellent, and sunscreen.

SAFETY

Usually, hiking with people you meet on the trail is a safe way to travel. Occasionally, however, you may meet someone who wants to hike with you but makes you feel ill-at-ease.
- Trust your instincts (women especially). Solo women hikers should be cautious about accepting male company.
- Keep an eye on your gear, especially expensive electronic equipment.
- Keep your options open—do not agree to pool gear such as cooking equipment or tents. You should be free to leave the partnership if you like.

Planning for the trail

The amount of planning you need to do varies according to the type and length of the trip, but drawing up an itinerary is an invaluable part of the process. In addition, you need to plan your proposed route carefully on a map, and estimate how far you will be hiking.

MAKING ITINERARIES

Itineraries are essential on longer backpacking trips because you need to calculate how much food to carry. In order to determine your food requirements, you need to know how many days it will take to get from one town to the next. Sometimes, all this means is dividing the total distance you will cover by the average daily distance you will travel. However, you may need to do more detailed planning on trails where there are few campsites or water sources, and in places where there are few opportunities to resupply. It is important to allow extra traveling time if you are intending to hike in areas where the climate or trail conditions could slow down your progress, or require you to take a detour. It is always useful to research your route, because some parks and reserves have permit regulations that require you to stay in designated areas at night, which will affect your itinerary.

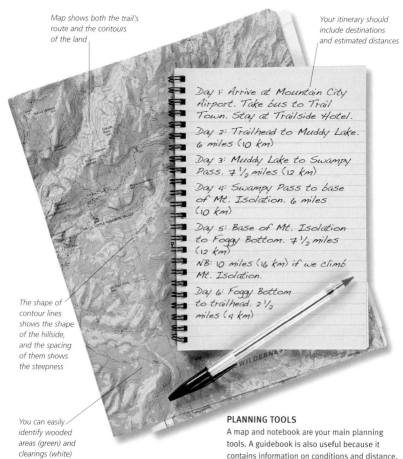

Map shows both the trail's route and the contours of the land

Your itinerary should include destinations and estimated distances

Day 1: Arrive at Mountain City Airport. Take bus to Trail Town. Stay at Trailside Hotel.

Day 2: Trailhead to Muddy Lake. 6 miles (10 km)

Day 3: Muddy Lake to Swampy Pass. 7 1/2 miles (12 km)

Day 4: Swampy Pass to base of Mt. Isolation. 6 miles (10 km)

Day 5: Base of Mt. Isolation to Foggy Bottom. 7 1/2 miles (12 km)
NB: 10 miles (16 km) if we climb Mt. Isolation.

Day 6: Foggy Bottom to trailhead. 2 1/2 miles (4 km)

The shape of contour lines shows the shape of the hillside, and the spacing of them shows the steepness

You can easily identify wooded areas (green) and clearings (white)

PLANNING TOOLS
A map and notebook are your main planning tools. A guidebook is also useful because it contains information on conditions and distance.

MARKING ROUTE INFORMATION

If you are hiking a named trail, your map work might consist simply of finding the route of the trail on your map. But in large parks and forests, you may have a large selection of trails from which to choose. After you have read the guidebook descriptions and selected a trail to hike, highlight it on your map to make navigating in the field much easier. In addition, highlight possible campsites, any long climbs, and all water sources.

MARKING A ROUTE

Highlighting your route with a highlighter allows you to see it easily while navigating in the field, and is especially useful in bad weather.

Follow the trail on the map that leads to a lodge and campsite

Using a transparent highligher allows you to mark the route without obscuring the map details

Note the position of the reservoir as a water source

MEASURING DISTANCE

To measure distance on a map, you can use either a map-measuring wheel or a thin piece of wire (*see below*). These kinds of measurement are at best an estimate. Small-scale maps give the least accurate result because the map cannot show all the twists and turns of the trail.

1 To measure distance on a map, simply take a thin piece of wire and try to bend it to match the route of the trail as closely as possible.

2 When you have traced the whole route, unbend the wire, measure it, and convert it, using the scale of the map (*see below*).

CALCULATING DISTANCE

When you have taken the measurement on the map, you will need to find out what distance it represents on the ground. On a scale of $2^1/_2$ inches—1 mile (or 1:25,000, 4 cm—1 km). When you place your wire against the scale on the map, you can read off the distance on the ground. When using small scale maps, you should add 10 percent as a safety margin, because they may not show short changes of direction.

USING A MAP

A map with route information marked will help you to reach your planned destination.

Preparing for hiking

Hiking on uneven ground or climbing and descending long inclines is more physically demanding than walking on pavement—especially while wearing hiking clothing and boots, and carrying a backpack. To prepare adequately, you need to try out your gear and get your body in shape.

Testing your gear and clothing

However wisely you choose your gear, you should still give it a test run. Take short practice hikes close to home to make sure your pack, clothing, and boots are comfortable. You should also familiarize yourself with new pieces of equipment and check that everything you will need fits into your backpack.

WALKING WITH YOUR BACKPACK

Take a few day hikes with your backpack fully loaded to make sure it fits properly and does not chafe or rub (*see* pp.26–7). Does it hurt after only a short while? Have you tried all the straps to see which ones help shift the weight of the load effectively? It is better to discover any problems before you find yourself in the middle of a long hike.

Hiking with a fully loaded pack can also cause your feet to swell, which may reveal any problems with the fit of your boots. Walking on roads with a backpack is no training for walking on rough trails, so find some uneven ground on which to test your boots and strengthen your ankles for rougher conditions.

TESTING YOUR CLOTHING

On training hikes, wear the clothing you plan to wear while hiking. You will soon notice if any seams are rubbing against your skin, if your top gets tucked up under the shoulder straps of your backpack, or if the legs of your shorts ride up and cause your thighs to chafe. Note the temperature, and whether the clothes you are wearing are comfortable. Ask yourself whether they will still be comfortable at the temperatures you expect to encounter on your hike.

TAKING A TRIAL RUN

If your gear and clothing work well on a short practice hike, you're less likely to encounter problems on a longer trail.

Adjust pack straps so that they are comfortable and not chafing

Check that hat feels secure and will not blow off in a strong wind

Check that pants do not chafe and allow enough leg mobility

After a long hike carrying a heavy load, boots should still feel comfortable

TESTING HARDWARE

Gadgets such as stoves, water filters, cameras, and GPS units take some time to learn to use. The more familiar you are with how your gear works, the more easily you will be able to use it—even in less-than-optimal conditions.

Before your hike, test your stove to be sure you have all its parts and everything is in working order. Similarly, be sure you know how your water filter works, and learn how to change or clean a water filter cartridge. Practice using a GPS unit at home and on a short hike (*see* p.81)—it will not help you to find your way if you do not know how to use it. If you are setting out with a new camera, test it first by shooting a roll of film in different lighting conditions. Finally, be sure to pack the instructions to any gear or gadgets you are not completely familiar with.

PACKING YOUR GEAR

Do not leave it until the last minute to pack your backpack. Check, for example, that your sleeping bag fits inside your backpack's sleeping bag compartment. If you have a bulky synthetic-fill sleeping bag and an ultralight small-capacity backpack, you could be in for a rude awakening. Keep size and space issues in mind when buying new gear.

Pack your backpack with everything you intend to take. Is there enough space for your tent? What about the tent poles? Where will your sleeping mat go? How much room will you need for all of your food? Is there a place for your water bottle and cooking equipment? Decide where each item goes and ensure that the pack is loaded and balanced comfortably, with no sharp objects poking against your back.

BREAKING IN YOUR HIKING BOOTS

Perhaps the most important way to prepare for a hike is to be absolutely certain that your boots and feet can coexist in comfort and harmony. Carrying a loaded backpack puts extra stress on your feet, and at the end of a day's hiking they may have swollen a size or more.

- Wear your boots around the house to double check the fit before breaking them in.
- Avoid blisters by going on short hikes to soften your boots and toughen your feet.

- Walk on uneven ground that forces your feet to bend in different directions.
- Wear wicking socks to remove sweat (which can exacerbate blisters).

- Wear thick, padded, woollen socks to add cushioning and avoid friction.
- Be sure to take blister treatment along, just in case your boots still rub.

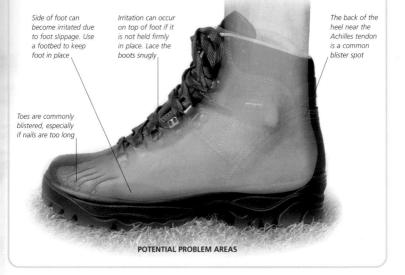

Side of foot can become irritated due to foot slippage. Use a footbed to keep foot in place

Irritation can occur on top of foot if it is not held firmly in place. Lace the boots snugly

The back of the heel near the Achilles tendon is a common blister spot

Toes are commonly blistered, especially if nails are too long

POTENTIAL PROBLEM AREAS

Conditioning your body for hiking

If you already participate in an ongoing fitness program, you will find your introduction to hiking much smoother than your more sedentary companions. Pre-hike training should include both aerobic exercise and weight training, as well as stretches for your leg, arm, and back muscles.

EXERCISING IN THE GYM

To hike up and down mountains—or even hills—with a pack on your back requires aerobic fitness. Training in a gym in advance to strengthen your heart, lungs, and leg muscles will pay off on the trail. If you are fit, you will be better prepared for the short-term exertion of climbing hills, and have the long-term endurance to hike all day.

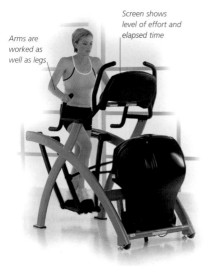

Arms are worked as well as legs

Screen shows level of effort and elapsed time

Adjustable weights build up leg strength

CROSS-COUNTRY SKI MACHINE

One of the most efficient ways of exercising is to use a cross-country ski machine, which works all muscle groups and provides aerobic conditioning.

WEIGHT TRAINING

Weight-bearing exercises strengthen muscles that will power you up hills. Look for exercises that work the quads, thighs, and hamstrings.

STRETCHING YOUR LEGS

Leg muscles bear the brunt of the work in hiking, and one of the chief complaints after a long day is leg stiffness. Stretching your legs regularly—both before and during your hike (*see* p.73)—can alleviate this. It can also help prevent injuries if you fall. Stretch calves, quads, thighs, and hamstrings.

HAMSTRING AND CALF

This exercise stretches the hamstring (the muscle at the back of the upper leg) and the calf (the back of the lower leg). Step one leg forward and flex the foot. Bend the other knee, lean forward and sit back into the position. Hold for a few seconds.

Place both hands above the bent knee to support your weight

Pulling the toes up stretches the back of the whole leg

Calf is stretched

STRETCHING YOUR UPPER BODY

The upper body may not seem to do much work in hiking, but arms and shoulders come into play when you are rock scrambling, or if you are using trekking poles. Stretching these muscles also stretches the back and neck, which can help alleviate pain and soreness.

SHOULDERS
Try to make your hands meet behind your back, and hold the position for a few seconds.

TRICEPS
Hold one elbow with the other hand and gently pull back, stretching the arm and back.

STRETCHING YOUR BACK

Back muscles can become stiff and sore from hiking with a heavy load. Stretching before your hike helps prepare your body for backpacking. When you are hiking, take time to stretch your back during rest breaks (*see* p.72) and at the end of the day.

BACK AND HAMSTRINGS
This stretch works both the back and legs. Be careful not to force any stretches, but rather gently lower yourself into a position that feels comfortable, then hold it for a few seconds.

Bend over gently and hold the stretch—do not bounce

Keep knees straight, but not rigidly locked

HIKING TIPS

ACCLIMATIZE YOURSELF
The conditions you will be hiking in may be different from those where you live. In particular, you will need time to get used to very cold or hot weather, and high altitudes.

■ Spend as much time outdoors as you can before your hike, even if the weather is poor.

■ In hot weather, be sure your first few days are slow paced with plenty of time for resting, as your feet will still be soft and prone to blistering. Drink and eat as often as possible to maintain your electrolyte balance, even if you are not thirsty or hungry.

■ At high altitudes, plan short break-in hikes before you start working hard. If hiking above 8,000 ft (2,400 m), limit elevation gain to 1,000 ft (300 m) per day. Also, try not to sleep more than 1,000 ft (300 m) higher than your previous campsite. Watch out for headaches and other symptoms of altitude sickness (*see* p.140), even at lower heights.

KNOW YOUR LIMITATIONS
It takes time to work up to long days and big climbs, so do not push yourself too far until you know what your body can do.

■ Take a rest break at least once an hour. Food, water, and rest can work miracles on drooping spirits and flagging energy.

■ Do not be afraid to slow down and alter your plans if it turns out that your original itinerary was too physcially ambitious.

Deciding what food to take

On short hikes, you need food to keep your energy levels high and to refresh you during breaks. On longer hikes, you still need the energy, but also need to be concerned with overall nutrition and food spoilage. There are many different foods that fit the bill—whether fresh or dried, ready to eat, or in need of cooking—and they all taste good in the fresh air after a long hike.

FOOD FOR DAY HIKES

Unless the weather is extremely hot, most food can survive a few hours in a daypack, so your choice is wide. Select a combination of foods that provide salts (important for rehydration), sugars (which provide a quick energy boost), and proteins and fats (for longer-term energy). Examples of good hiking foods include fresh and dried fruit, wholegrain bread, cheese, peanut butter, nuts, dried meat, and energy bars.

In high temperatures, pack food such as cheese and meat in the center of your pack to keep them cool. Avoid carrying foods that spoil easily, such as anything containing mayonnaise, sandwiches with watery ingredients such as tomatoes, or spread-type fillings, which can make bread soggy. Put foods that crumble and crush easily (such as cookies and crackers) in plastic containers with lids.

FOOD FOR OVERNIGHT HIKES

In addition to the lunches and snacks carried by day-hikers, you will need to take dinner and breakfast. Choose meals that need the least cooking. The easiest dinners to prepare are one-pot meals such as stews or pasta dishes, or prepackaged freeze-dried foods. Foods that are somewhat soupy in texture help to replenish water and so help to prevent dehydration. For breakfast, eat hot or cold cereals, with or without dried milk and sugar, or granola or energy bars.

DRIED FRUIT

CEREAL

CRACKERS

CHEESE

PASTA   **POTATO GRANULES**

NUTS   **CHOCOLATE**

PACKING FOOD

To cut down both weight and bulk, remove food from its original packaging whenever possible, but keep any wrappers that have cooking instructions on them. Repack the food in ziplocking plastic bags and store them in a waterproof stuff sack.

TEA BAGS

ELECTROLYTE REPLACEMENT DRINK

HOW MUCH FOOD TO PACK?

The amount of food required for a day hike varies according to your metabolism and how far you hike. As a rule of thumb, however, 2 lb (900 g) of mostly dried food is ample for one full day (three meals plus snacks) of hiking. On short, warm weather hikes, you may not need quite so much food. However, if you intend to cover long distances in cold weather, you may need as much as 25 per cent more.

NUT BAR

BREAKFAST

Some hikers eat instant oatmeal, dried fruit, cereal, or nut or fruit bars for a quick no-fuss, no-cook breakfast. Others like to prepare for the day ahead with a fully cooked meal, such as the dehydrated egg and pancake mixes available from outdoor retailers. Coffee and tea can be made using a camping stove, although caffeinated drinks are diuretics, so are not recommended in hot weather.

SALAMI   **BAGEL**

LUNCH

Your midday meal should require no preparation or cooking, and should be convenient to eat even if it is raining. You may prefer not to take lunch at all but rather eat several small snacks during the day. Cheese, salami, dried meat, yeast extract, or peanut butter sandwiches, and crackers, bagels, and pitta bread are all good lunch foods.

CANNED MEAT   **GRAVY GRANULES**

DINNER

There are three main choices of food for an evening meal: home-cooked food that you have dehydrated and packed for the trail, prepacked freeze-dried or quick-cook foods such as mashed potato, or fresh ingredients cooked on a stove. Examples include pasta with tomato sauce, macaroni cheese, and instant rice with gravy granules and a can of meat.

ENERGY BAR

SNACKS

Energy bars, developed specifically for endurance athletes, are popular among hikers—and so are chocolate bars containing nuts and fruit. Other choices are nuts, dried fruit, pretzels, and cereal bars. Pack several helpings of snacks, because you will enjoy having them during breaks throughout the day, as well as for dessert at lunch and dinnertime.

HOT CHOCOLATE   **DRIED COFFEE**

DRINKS

Hot drinks are ideal for cold weather, although it is better to choose decaffeinated rather than caffeinated beverages. Tea, coffee, and hot chocolate are all popular. Also, cold electrolyte-replacement drinks can keep you going in hot weather by replacing lost sugars and salts. Carry plenty of water with you, and keep it easily accessible so you can sip it as you walk to avoid dehydration.

ON THE
TRAIL

All about walking

Novice hikers are often surprised at how much effort it takes to hike a trail. Your lungs and heart must work harder to climb hills and carry a pack, muscles can become stiff and sore, and feet can be blistered by new boots. By taking it slowly, you can minimize these problems.

Walking with ease

It is the steep slopes and rough tracks that make trail hiking so much more arduous than walking. Uneven terrain, rocks, and mud all interfere with foot placement and rhythm, and climbing a hill requires much more effort while carrying a pack. This makes hiking both a challenge and excellent exercise. A few techniques can help you move more easily and efficiently.

PACING YOURSELF

A novice hiker may be tempted to walk too quickly, pause for breath, then set off again at the same fast speed. More experienced hikers make steady progress because they choose a pace that they can sustain all day. This pace may be much slower than they would walk on a city street, but it is one that enables them to walk steadily uphill and around obstacles while carrying a pack. The key is not to become out of breath—if you can hold a conversation while walking uphill, you have found the right pace.

TAKING REST BREAKS

Resting at regular intervals helps you to conserve energy for later in the day. Rest breaks are also opportunities to snack, drink water, check your feet for blisters, and stretch (*see* pp.72–5). At first, plan to stop once every hour for about 10 minutes. As you gain experience, you might want to alter your schedule of walking and resting.

WALKING CONTINUOUSLY

Although rest breaks are desirable, it is not always possible to stop for them. In cold or wet weather, 10-minute breaks once an hour may be dangerous, as they can increase the risk of hypothermia. In such cases, you need to adjust for the conditions so that you do not need to rest. Wear one more layer of clothing than normal, and walk a little more slowly. The extra layer will keep you warm even though you are exercising less strenuously, and the slower pace will allow you to continue longer without resting. Add or remove gloves or a hat to fine tune your body temperature without stopping.

KEEPING A STEADY PACE

A slow, steady pace is easier to maintain over a long day than short, fast bursts followed by frequent rests.

USING THE REST STEP

Sometimes a hill is so steep that you cannot climb it without constantly stopping—no matter how slowly you are hiking. In such cases, the "rest step" is an invaluable technique. At first it will seem like an awkward start-and-stop motion, but, if done correctly, it will enable you to hike steeply uphill for long distances without stopping.

1 Begin the rest step from a stationary upright position. Step forward with your right leg. Keep the weight on the left (back) leg, with the knee locked. Pause before taking the next step, with the weight still on your back leg.

2 Transfer the weight to your right leg. Push yourself up with your right leg and swing your left leg forward to take the next step. Lock your right knee, so that the right leg is bearing all of your weight. Pause with your weight on your right leg.

3 Now transfer the weight to your left leg. Push yourself up with your left leg and swing your right leg forward to take the next step. Continue climbing in this fashion, and you should be walking at a slow, steady pace.

EATING AND DRINKING ON THE TRAIL

You must eat and drink regularly, and should carry a variety of snacks—both sweet and salty. High-sugar snacks give you a quick burst of energy, while dried fruits and nuts (*see* pp.66–7) provide longer-lasting energy release. Always have enough water on hand to drink, and know where the next source of water is.

WATER FOR DRINKING
Try to make a habit of drinking at every rest stop, even if you are not thirsty—adequate hydration is important in any kind of weather. If you are sweating frequently, electrolyte drinks help to balance your body.

CHECKLIST

SNACKS

Take along a variety of both sweet and salty snacks, such as:
- cereal bars
- nuts
- dried fruit
- chocolate
- energy bars.

DRINKS

You should have at least one of the following easily available when hiking:
- water
- powdered electrolyte replacement drinks.

You should avoid:
- caffeinated drinks such as coffee, tea, and carbonated drinks (they are diuretics, which contribute to dehydration).

Avoiding stiffness

Walking with a heavy backpack on uneven terrain for long distances means your muscles will be stressed in unfamiliar ways—even very fit people usually feel stiff after the first day's hike.

By using a few minutes of your rest breaks to stretch, you can keep yourself limber and reduce stiffness. Here are some exercises that stretch the muscles that are most likely to become stiff.

BACK AND NECK STRETCH

The back and neck can feel tight and stiff from the pressure of carrying a pack. You can use your pack's load lifters, stabilizer adjusters, chest strap, and shoulder straps to vary the pressure on your shoulders, neck, and hips while walking. However, it is still a good idea to stretch whenever you have a break.

WHAT TO STRETCH

The following muscles can become tired and sore from unaccustomed exercise and strain:
- the back from carrying a load
- the calves from climbing uphill
- the quads from uphills and downhills
- the hamstrings from hiking uphill

A towel will work as well as a t-shirt

Reach high and feel the stretch in your arms

Adopt a relaxed, comfortable stance

Feel a pull in your shoulders and chest

1 Take a piece of clothing, such as a large t-shirt. Hold each end and stretch it out in front of you.

2 Make a sweeping arc with your arms, bringing them forward, then up over your head.

3 Bend your arms and take the clothing down behind your head, holding it straight in both hands.

INNER THIGH AND QUAD STRETCH

The inner thigh and quad muscles may become exhausted from long climbs.

1 Kneel in a deep lunge. Push the knee of your back leg to the ground to stretch the quad muscle.

2 Put both hands on the ground to the inside of your front leg. Push the knee of your front leg outward, to stretch the groin and inner thigh muscles. Repeat the exercise with the other leg in front.

The back is kept straight, but not stiff

Keep the neck relaxed, but do not drop your head

Keep your arms straight

Push the leg away from the body

HAMSTRING STRETCH

Hamstrings power much of your walking, especially uphill.

1 Sit on the ground with your legs spread wide apart, keeping the knees relaxed. Bend at the waist and reach forward as far as you can toward one foot.

Try not to round your back too much, but stretch your chest toward your thigh

Stretch the leg only as far as it will comfortably go

2 Now move your torso so that you are leaning forward and reaching straight ahead of you.

Keep your shoulders relaxed as you bend forward

Flex your feet and point toes upward

Press your chest toward the ground

Place your hands on the ground and walk them forward

3 Finally, stretch out over your other leg, keeping your knees relaxed.

Avoid tensing your shoulders and neck

Stretch forward as far as you can without straining

Taking care of your feet

Your feet bear both your weight and the weight of your pack. Carrying this weight, wearing new boots, and ignoring "hot spots" all contribute to blisters. Keep your feet clean and dry, make sure your boots fit comfortably, and stop at the first sign of a blister. The key to an enjoyable hike is prevention.

AVOIDING BLISTERS

The first rule of foot care is to stop and check your feet as soon as you feel even a small amount of pain. It takes only a few seconds for a barely noticeable area of inflammation to turn into a fully-fledged blister, so the sooner you react, the better. Even a single grain of sand lodged in a sock can cause a blister if it is not removed quickly. Hikers are often reluctant to stop for a mere feeling of discomfort, especially if this means their hiking partners must stop as well. But preventing a blister is perhaps the most important thing you can do to ensure an enjoyable hike. If a blister has already begun to form, treat the "hot spot" immediately (see p.134).

LOOKING FOR BLISTERS
Check feet for blisters at rest stops—look for red areas, especially at the back of the heel and on the toes where your boots are most likely to rub.

CHECKING YOUR FEET

Even if you do not feel any problems, you should check your feet during at least some of your rest stops. Do this until you are confident that you will be aware of a blister in the early stages. Taking off your socks and shoes during rest stops gives your feet a chance to dry and air, which in turn helps to prevent blisters.

WASHING YOUR FEET

A refreshing soak in cool water will remove tiny grains of dirt that could rub against your skin and cause blisters. It also rejuvenates the muscles in your feet. Make sure that you dry your feet thoroughly before putting your socks and boots back on.

CARING FOR YOUR FEET
Rinsing your feet not only feels good and cools them down, it cleans away any grains of dirt, sand, or grass seeds.

FOOT CARE TIPS

Get into the habit of taking care of your feet. A few simple routines can help keep them blister-free.

■ A thin moisture-wicking liner sock should be worn next to the skin, with a thicker cushioning sock made of wool or a wool blend over the top. If your boots feel too tight, try a lighter-weight sock (see p.21).

■ Boots come with liners already in place, but you can add to or replace them with thicker, stronger insoles to improve the fit of your boots.

■ Experiment with different ways of lacing your boots to give more room or to keep the boot more firmly in place (see below).

■ Sharp toenails can rub against adjacent toes, causing blisters, so trim your nails regularly.

■ If you know that a certain part of your foot is prone to blistering, pre-treat the area by covering it with a piece of moleskin or an adhesive bandage.

■ Keep your feet and socks as clean as possible. Hikers often reuse the thick cushioning socks for two (or more) days, but rinse out the lighter, liner socks, which are worn next to the skin. This removes dirt that can contribute to blistering.

AIRING SOCKS

Keep your socks as clean as possible. If you will be reusing the same socks for several days (which is common among experienced hikers), air them whenever possible.

AIRING ON HIKING POLES

ADJUSTING YOUR BOOTS

Boot laces can be adjusted in various ways to make your feet feel more comfortable. You may have to readjust the lacing several times during the day, as your feet sweat and swell, or as they gradually work the laces loose. Tightening the lacing can keep your feet from moving around too much, and it gives more support to the bones and muscles in your feet and ankles. Loosening the laces relieves pressure.

AVOIDING TIGHT TOES
Loosen the laces to give more room in a tight toe area, but double the laces over at the arch to keep the boot from slipping.

ADJUSTING LOOSE BOOTS
Tighten the bootlaces around the forefoot if the boot feels too loose. Also tighten them if your forefoot feels unstable in any way.

SECURING LACES
To keep laces from loosening at the top, lace them across the top of the hooks first so that they cross over themselves.

Finding your way

A map is an aerial view of the landscape. It not only tells you where you are, but also tells you what kind of terrain lies ahead. Using maps and a compass correctly will tell you what to expect on the other side of the next mountain, as well as just around the next corner.

Learning to read maps

A wide variety of maps is available to the hiker, from hand-drawn squiggles presented by fellow hikers to detailed contour maps. The wilder and more rugged the trek, the more detailed your maps need to be. Maps suitable for hiking use a much larger scale than road maps, to show sufficient detail.

CONTOUR MAPS

The most common maps used by hikers are contour maps (also known as topographic maps), which use a series of lines joining places of equal height to indicate the contours of the land.

Exposed ridge ending in an incline

Long, flat lines that are close together indicate a wall-like incline with few, if any, breaks that can be climbed. The trail is likely to traverse here

Contour lines close together show a steep incline, which may be difficult to hike

Long contour lines indicate a ridge. When they converge in a series of U-shapes, one within the next, the ridge is ending in an incline

A figure-eight shape indicates a saddle between two peaks

A series of circles shows a summit, knob, or protrusion; the dense lines on one side of it show a steep incline on that side

A lake surrounded by close lines is an unlikely campsite because the sides are too steep

FEATURES ON A CONTOUR MAP

Many topographical features you see on a contour map are easy to recognize—hills, valleys, saddles, and ridges all have characteristic contour patterns. Interpreting a map correctly is the key to finding a safe route.

HOW TO READ A CONTOUR MAP

A contour map shows information on the ground such as peaks and valleys, as well as rivers, lakes, roads, trails, buildings, and power lines. A key of symbols will tell you how to interpret the signs for natural and artificial features. Reading a contour map is just like reading any other map. The only difference is the use of contour lines to show the elevation of the land.

CHOOSING A SCALE

Look for maps that have a scale of from 1:25,000 ($2\frac{1}{2}$ inches on the map equals 1 mile on the ground, or 4 cm on the map equals 1 km on the ground) to 1:50,000. The bigger the second number, the more area the map will cover, but the less detail it will show.

Steep incline that is part of a peak

Long traverse with few breaks

Saddle between two peaks

Steep-sided protrusion

Steep lakeside location

The hiking route avoids a climb and provides a safe passage around the peaks, following the route of the stream

FEATURES IN THE LANDSCAPE

The features identified on the contour map translate into the landscape above. Learn to recognize characteristic contour patterns on your map and visualize them as actual features in the landscape.

MAP SOFTWARE

Computerized maps for many hiking areas are available through the internet or on CD-Roms. Electronic maps frequently offer much more information than paper maps. They even allow you to compare several different routes, adding up total elevation gains and distance from campsite to campsite. When available, these programs can be an enormous help when you are planning longer hikes.

MAP ESSENTIALS

MEASURING MAP DISTANCES

Being able to look at a map and accurately gauge the distance from one point to another is an essential skill. There are two ways you can do this:

■ **Use a map wheel**—this is a tiny wheel that you trace precisely along the route you plan to take. The wheel measures the distance on the map, which can then be scaled up to an on-the-ground distance.

Distance in miles is shown in the window

Hold the device like a pen and roll the wheel along route on the map

MAP WHEEL

■ **Estimate distance**—split the route into sections by marking the map with a pencil each time the route turns. Measure each section with a ruler, add the figures up, then convert to miles.

■ **The total distance** that you calculate will probably be less than the actual distance. This is because neither method above can account for the extra distance caused by climbing and descending.

■ **The more detailed** the map, the more accurate your estimate will be. For example, switchbacks are often drawn inaccurately but add great distance. If your trail is shown as a squiggly line crossing steep contours, add 30 percent to your estimate.

Using a map and compass

A compass is a simple instrument that points to magnetic north. With this information and a contour map, you can orientate yourself. Using a map and compass quickly and confidently takes a little practice, but it is an essential skill that will pay off time and again as you make your way through the countryside and when hiking off marked trails.

HOW A COMPASS WORKS

A compass is nothing more than a needle floating in water or oil. The end of the needle is magnetically charged, and it points to magnetic north, which is the place where the planet's magnetic lines of force converge.

Orientating arrow moves with the rotating dial

Magnifying-glass

Direction of travel arrow

Base plate

Orientating lines

Rotating dial

Magnetic needle

Clinometer measures angles of inclination

FINDING YOUR WAY

This compass allows you to work out a bearing, set the dial, and use the compass as a direction finder.

ORIENTATING MAP AND COMPASS

To find a bearing and an exact location, you need first to orientate your map correctly with the aid of your compass.

FINDING NORTH

Align your compass with the map gridlines. Rotate map and compass until the needle is aligned with the "N" marked on the movable dial. Adjust for declination.

READY TO NAVIGATE

The map is now lined up with the landscape, and you can determine all other directions and find your position by triangulating *(see right)*.

UNDERSTANDING DECLINATION

While the needle of a compass points to magnetic north, the "north" shown on maps is known as "grid north." The difference between magnetic north and grid north is known as declination, or magnetic variation. The number of degrees (east or west) should be printed on the map. Rotate your compass dial clockwise (for west) or counterclockwise (for east) to find grid north. Without adjustment, the discrepancy between the two norths will accumulate and could put you many miles off route.

Magnetic north   Grid north

TURN DIAL CLOCKWISE FOR DECLINATION WEST

FINDING A BEARING

This means finding the direction between your position and a fixed identifiable object. It is best to choose something that can be easily identified on a map, such as a distinctive hill. This is a useful skill because you can use two bearings to locate your position on a map (*see below*).

Landmark
Select a landmark that is easily identifiable on your map, such as a house, church, or distinctive landform

FINDING THE BEARING TO AN OBJECT
Point the direction of travel arrow toward the object. Find north, then adjust for declination by turning the dial by the correct number of degrees west or east. The direction of travel arrow will now point to your bearing on the compass dial.

Your bearing
The degrees on your compass dial give your bearing to that object

---

USING TRIANGULATION

Triangulation is the practice of taking two different bearings and seeing where they intersect on the map. By identifying two features in the field and on the map, you can locate your position on the map. You will need to add or subtract the magnetic variation in order to put the correct bearing on the map. Where the two lines intersect is your location. Taking a third bearing will pinpoint your position more accurately.

FINDING YOUR POSITION

Find a bearing from your position to the first feature, remembering to adjust for declination (*see above*). Next, find the feature on your map. Without rotating the compass dial, place your compass on the map so that the direction of travel arrow points to the feature on the map. Orientate your compass to the map (*see left*). Then, using one of the long edges of the compass (these run parallel to the direction of travel arrow), draw a line from the feature back toward you. Your location is somewhere along this line. Repeat the process with a new feature, which should be at roughly a 90-degree angle to the first. The point at which the two lines intersect is your position.

Orientating the map
Let the edge of your compass touch your landmark. Turn the map and compass (together), so the magnetic needle points to true north

Draw a line along the edge of your compass from the landmark back toward yourself

Using other navigation methods

In addition to the traditional map and compass, there are other methods that you can use to find your way when hiking. Some of these natural signposts are as old as the stars, while others are as new as satellites. In fact, both stars and satellites can be used to keep you on the right-path.

NATURE SHOWS THE WAY

There are natural indicators that, if you are aware of them, can help you to find your way. By paying attention to where and how plants and vegetation grow, you can glean information to help you to determine direction. These indicators are not fail-safe, but, taken collectively, they can be used to help point you in the right direction.

Some plants, for example, lean toward the sun (to the south in the northern hemisphere; to the north in the southern hemisphere). Likewise, vegetation is thicker on the sunny side of a hill (south in the northern hemisphere, and north in the southern hemisphere). The bark of a tree will feel warmer to the touch on the sunny side, which again indicates direction depending on the hemisphere.

TREE TIP
In the northern hemisphere, moss grows on the north sides of trees in dry areas. In the southern hemisphere, the opposite effect can be observed.

PLANT POINTERS
Barrel cacti in the American Southwest are among the plants that grow tilted toward the sun. Other plants, such as sunflowers, turn to face the sun during the day.

USING THE STARS

If you are in the northern hemisphere, you can use the North Star to locate north. To find it, you first need to locate the Big Dipper, then follow the line made by the two stars that form the front end of its "cup." These point to the North Star (Polaris), which always lies directly over north on the horizon.

In the southern hemisphere, you can use the Southern Cross to find south. Below the cross, toward the horizon, you will find two bright stars. Imagine a line running perpendicular from the mid-point between them. Draw another line from the long axis of the Southern Cross. The point where these two lines intersect lies over south on the horizon.

THE BIG DIPPER
This is one of the easiest constellations to identify in the northern sky. Four stars make the "cup," and three more form the "handle" of the Dipper.

THE SOUTHERN CROSS
As distinctive in the southern sky as the Big Dipper is in the northern, the Southern Cross comprises four stars that form the shape of a kite or cross.

STAYING ON COURSE

Stay focused on your route—the more monotonous the terrain, the more you need to pay attention, because lack of concentration could cause you to wander. As you travel along the trail, there are things you can do to make sure you stay on the right route. Most are pure common sense, but they are still worth noting.

Start by looking at your map before you set out, and identifying prominent features you expect to pass or see in the near distance. Mentally check them off as you spot them. If you see a landmark that you were not expecting to see, it could be an indication that you have veered off course. Stop and check your map.

Confirm your direction with your body's shadow as you walk—if you are walking north in the northern hemisphere, your shadow should be to your right in the afternoon. Keep track of the time you have been walking and your estimated pace. If you become lost, being able to accurately estimate the distance you have walked can be helpful in determining your position.

CHECKING YOUR POSITION
Pay attention to your surroundings as you hike. To be sure of your position, continually check your map for landmarks, to make sure that what you see matches what the map says you should see.

USING A WATCH

You can use a watch in conjunction with the sun to get an accurate indication of north and south (depending on which hemisphere you are in). This technique is most reliable when you can see the sun, but if it is cloudy, you can align your watch with the brightest area of sky.

NORTHERN HEMISPHERE

Look for the sun and line it up with the hour hand. South lies halfway between the hour hand and 12 o'clock.

SOUTHERN HEMISPHERE

Look for the sun and line it up with the 12 o'clock mark. North lies halfway between 12 o'clock and the hour hand.

USING GPS

A Global Positioning System (GPS) receives signals from multiple satellites, which can be used to accurately calculate your position to within a few feet.

■ The GPS takes a reading of where you are. If you punch in the coordinates of your destination, the unit will point in the direction of travel.

■ GPS is especially valuable for navigating in thick fog or in terrain where easily identifiable topographic features are few and far between.

■ Before leaving a place to which you intend to return, note the coordinates. If you get lost, you can simply enter the coordinates and the GPS will lead you back there.

■ If the trail changes direction, you can enter the coordinates of intermediate stages, known as "waypoints." You can even do this before you start your trip.

■ Use GPS coordinates in an emergency to send messages to rescuers about your location.

Signal is bounced off a satellite

Multiple signals allow GPS to show your position

SATELLITE LINK

Hiking in difficult terrain

Hiking could be described as the art of going around obstacles, but sometimes there is no option but to find a way across areas of difficult terrain such as boulder fields, rock scrambles, snow, and ice. As you gain experience, however, crossing these obstacles becomes easier.

Crossing rocky ground

Good balance, attention to footing, the ability to find a safe route, and confidence on steep terrain are all vital to hiking on rocky ground.

Do not be discouraged if your first foray is difficult—it will become easier with experience and by following a few basic techniques.

HIKING THROUGH LARGE BOULDERS
Look for the line of least resistance, and use your trekking poles to help you pick your way down any tricky steps and drops.

USING TREKKING POLES
Walking on rocky, uneven ground is a skill that takes practice, especially if the slope is steep or there are large boulders or loose rocks underfoot. Trekking poles will help you to keep your balance in each of these situations, whether hiking uphill or downhill. They also allow you to hike more efficiently, by transferring some of the effort of climbing on to your arms and shoulders. Using poles will also reduce the shock of each footfall on your joints when you are going downhill.

DESCENDING WITH TREKKING POLES
Trekking poles transfer weight from the legs to the arms, relieving stress on knees. They also help with balance on large downhill steps and boulders.

Walk slowly and test each rock before placing your full weight on it

On even ground, lean forward to place your bodyweight on the poles

Grip the pole securely but lightly to avoid jarring your wrist

Keep your arms bent at 90 degrees

Where possible, move one pole forward and step through with the opposite leg

SCRAMBLING

Some trails require you to use your hands and legs to scramble up rocks. Wear footwear with good traction and choose an internal frame pack that hugs the body. Transfer to your backpack items that you usually carry on your front. Pack heavier items toward the bottom, close to your back, to improve your balance, and secure your trekking poles to your pack.

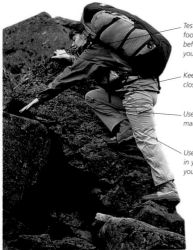

Test hand- and footholds for security before committing your weight

Keep your lower body close to the rock

Use your hands to help maintain your balance

Use the large muscles in your legs to support your weight

TESTING A HANDHOLD   **FINDING A SAFE FOOTHOLD**

SCRAMBLING UP ROCKS

Always maintain three points of contact with the rock, and test the next hand- or foothold to be sure it will support your full bodyweight, before you move your hand or foot onto it.

ASSESSING SCRAMBLING GRADES

Use the techniques on this page to tackle terrain rated up to US grade 3. Routes of US grade 4 and above require specialized climbing equipment and techniques.

YOSEMITE DECIMAL SYSTEM

1 Normal hiking on uneven, rocky terrain.
2 Easy scramble with occasional use of hands.
3 Full use of hands, with some exposure.
4 Technical moves required. Rope needed, rock-climbing skills will help.

HIKING

■ **Know your limits.** The allure of reaching a summit is powerful, but it is important to set a time at which you turn around in order to return safely before dark. Make sure you have enough energy to make the return trip, as reaching the top is only half of the route—the other, more hazardous half, is descending to the bottom.

■ **Keep an eye on the weather.** Conditions change rapidly in mountainous country, which may make continuing your route dangerous or impossible.

SCRAMBLING

■ **Keep your cool.** Exposed rock ledges, small hand- and footholds, and large rocks can frighten even experienced trekkers. When facing difficulty, take a moment to catch your breath and calm down, then study your route options.

■ **If hiking with a partner,** do not push them into doing something unsafe. The knife-edge ridge that feels secure to you might seem like a precarious tightrope to your partner. If they find it difficult, help them by pointing out an easier route, or carry your partner's pack. Be encouraging, but respect their limitations.

■ **Check that there** is a way to turn back. This is especially important when descending obstacles that you might have to reascend later. If necessary, leave a rope in place.

BOULDER HOPPING

When hiking through rocky terrain, you can use speed and momentum to your advantage by boulder hopping. The basic principle is to hop lightly from boulder to boulder using your arms or trekking poles to stay balanced. Practice without a pack on medium-sized, stable rocks. If you need to carry a backpack, pack as little as possible, since the heavier the pack the more likely you are to jar your knees.

CROSSING A BOULDER FIELD
Pick your route by looking ahead for a series of evenly sized boulders. Larger boulders are more stable, but may require more effort to climb.

Look several paces ahead to plan your route

Use your hands to stay balanced

Keep your knees bent and relaxed

If you begin to lose your balance, continue forward, stepping lightly from foot to foot until you regain your equilibrium

MOVING ACROSS BOULDERS
Boulder hopping is a high-speed method of negotiating difficult terrain quickly and safely.

TRAVERSING SCREE

Scree is the mass of fine, small rocks that is often found above the treeline on mountain slopes. It slides underfoot, particularly as the angle of the slope increases. Walking on scree can be likened to trying to climb a descending escalator—for every step you take up the slope, you may slide two steps back down. But with experience, and by using the techniques shown below, hiking on scree can be exhilarating and fun.

CROSSING SCREE
Control your momentum by looking for a zig-zag path that passes over scree and consists of rocks of approximately the same size.

WALKING SIDEWAYS
Traverse scree by walking sideways step by step. This will provide more contact between the long side of your foot and the slope to give stability.

CLIMBING ON SCREE

If possible, walk near the edge of the scree slope where you are more likely to find large, stable boulders. If you are forced to walk in the middle of a scree slope, look for larger rocks that may be tightly wedged into the slope, since they are less likely to slip when you put your full weight on them. Test large rocks for stability by placing your weight on them gradually, but be particularly cautious if they are lodged in smaller scree.

Pack hoisted high on back

Arm raised to maintain balance

Foot lifted high to swing boot hard

Fine scree allows steps to be kicked

Leg bent at knee to support body

FEET SPREAD-EAGLED
Climb with your feet splayed, putting weight on the instep of each boot. Take small steps to reduce the strain on your legs and the chance of slipping.

KICKING STEPS
Keeping your bodyweight centered, kick your boots nose-first into the scree slope. Stay relaxed, but be prepared to steady yourself if you slip.

DESCENDING ON SCREE

"Screeing" is a technique where you let gravity do the work for you—by descending in a style that is part sliding and part slow-motion jogging. It is one of the most exhilarating ways to descend a mountain. Fine, deep scree is required to avoid twisting an ankle, tripping, or injuring yourself on the large rocks that sometimes poke out of mountainsides. You will find suitable scree on the upper slopes of most hills, mountains, and volcanoes. To avoid getting small rocks in your boots, secure your pants to your boots with strong tape, or wear gaiters that cover the top of your boots.

STARTING THE DESCENT
Launch yourself down the slope, starting with short, gentle hops as if jogging in slow motion.

SLIDING DOWNHILL
Dig your heel into the slope and use your momentum to slide a short distance with each footfall.

RIGHTING YOURSELF
Use your hands to steady yourself in case you lose your balance. Relax your knees and keep moving.

Crossing water

Water crossings can be among the most challenging obstacles you will face, especially in late spring, when mountain snow melts into streams and rivers. Water can also become an obstacle on shoreline hikes (especially during high tide), or when hiking through waterlogged ground alongside marshes and bogs. Ensure that you cross rivers, bogs, and tidal flats safely.

THE BEST TIME TO CROSS

Try to plan major crossings as early in the day as possible. During snowmelt in the spring, rivers run slower in the early morning, because the melt-off slows during the colder nighttime hours.

CHOOSING A PLACE TO CROSS

The best place to cross a stream or river is usually found by following the trail to the water's edge. But in late spring and early summer, when the river is running at its highest, the situation may be entirely different—do not assume the trail is leading to the safest crossing. Avoid the turbulence that causes white water—the safest river crossings are where the water is calm and no deeper than hip-high. Look for these conditions around river bends, where the stream widens and slows to make the turn. Note that the darker (and greener) the water, the deeper it is, and there may be a powerful current. Make sure that the bank on the far side is not steep or undercut, which could make it difficult for you to climb out of the water.

SITUATIONS TO AVOID

White water is always dangerous and should never be crossed—if you trip or your feet catch on rocks while crossing, the force of the water could cause you to drown. Avoid crossing upstream of rapids or waterfalls—these should be noted on a good map.

If you are hiking with someone who is reluctant to cross, offer to carry their backpack across. If they are still unwilling, do not try to persuade them; turn back or find an easier crossing.

A SAFE CROSSING-POINT
During times of high water, evaluate the conditions. If they appear dangerous, walk upstream in search of safer options, and always cross with caution.

WADING ACROSS WITH TREKKING POLES
Trekking poles can help you to keep your balance. In a fast-running stream, face diagonally upstream, as this helps to control the effect of the river's current.

WADING ACROSS A RIVER

Wading is often the safest option when crossing moving water. Always face upstream, diagonal to the current, when crossing. If you are carrying sports sandals, wear them to protect your feet. If not, take off your socks and remove your boot liners. Put your boots back on and wade across. To help keep your balance, use trekking poles for support. It may help to unbuckle your backpack's hip belt and loosen the shoulder straps, so that you can shrug it off if you fall.

If you are crossing in a group, put the strongest hikers at the ends and link arms. Move slowly across in a line, diagonal to the river's current.

WOODEN BRIDGES

Test bridges for stability and cross carefully, one person at a time. They may be unstable and, if wet, very slippery.

ROCK HOPPING

A technique that can get you across with dry feet, rock hopping is best carried out using trekking poles for balance. Pick the route first and evaluate the steps you will take. Decide which rocks are obviously stable, and which might be slippery.

Test your steps before committing your weight. If you have already committed to a step and it turns out to be unstable, move quickly to the next step, using your poles for balance. If you start losing your balance, remember that stepping into the water is an option. It is better to step into the river and get wet feet than fall into it.

CROSSING A WOODEN BRIDGE

Wooden bridges range from well-engineered construction projects to logs placed across a stream. Always test a bridge first to see if it is fixed at either end and to assess its stability. Never cross on a log jam—it takes only a little weight to dislodge the logs. If the bridge is too narrow or unstable to walk on, try shuffling across in a sitting position.

CROSSING WITH ROPES

Unless you are trained in river rescue, do not use a hand-held rope to cross a river. However, if a rope is fixed in place, it can give added security. Hold on to it, standing on the downstream side to avoid getting tangled in the rope if you lose your balance. Do not use a karabiner (a metal clip) to attach yourself to the rope—if you fall, you could be held underwater by the force of the current.

CROSSING WATERLOGGED GROUND

Most hiking trails avoid bogs, marshland, and areas prone to quicksand. These areas are all made up of waterlogged ground, so with each step you take, you will sink further into mud or sand.

If there is no other way round, look for a route through. Wet ground is uneven, and the footsteps of previous hikers can tell you how deep and hard the soil is. Aim for natural hard spots in the soft ground. Look for trees and shrubs that grow on larger, harder pieces of ground. Large rocks are a solid place to tread, and thick tussocks of hard grass also make good footholds.

Trails that pass through waterlogged ground often rely on puncheons. These are bridges formed of short wooden posts set vertically in the ground. Bridges formed of fallen logs may also exist.

If you start to sink in mud or quicksand, try to run across, using any logs, tussocks of grass, or rocks as safe zones. If you fall in, remember it is just saturated ground. Stay afloat with a swimming motion until you work out where you can scramble out. Look for tussocks of grass, logs, or rocks to cling onto.

SAFETY IN WET GROUND
When ground becomes saturated, the suction of mud pulls at your boots. You should wear tightly laced, ankle-high boots in such conditions.

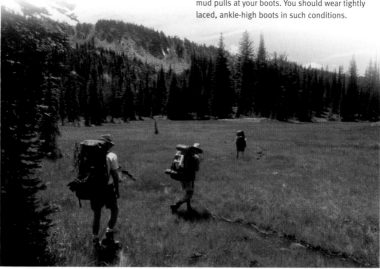

CROSSING TIDAL FLATS

You may encounter areas of mud and sand that are exposed at low tide and flooded at high tide when following coastal and estuarine trails over tidal flats. You must avoid coming across one of these areas at high tide, only to be unable to cross it until hours later. Guidebooks will tell you where you need to be concerned about tidal crossings. Use this in conjunction with a local tide table, which will tell you the times of high and low tides. Usually, you will have a safe window of several hours in which to cross both ways. Cross in bare feet or wearing sports sandals, as the damp sand will soak your boots even at low tide.

SAFETY ON TIDAL FLATS
You can only cross tidal flats at low tide, which occurs once a day. Be particularly careful of planning a crossing when the tide is rising.

Crossing snow and ice

Water in frozen form can be every bit as treacherous as flowing water. Hikers in high mountains may encounter ice and snow all summer long. Snowfields can be especially challenging in late spring and early summer, when they may be extremely slippery, especially on the northern slopes of mountains.

HIKING TRAILS AND SNOW

Snow usually lingers in the same places each year, so hiking trails are generally routed around these obstacles. However, in years of high snowfall, you may find yourself confronted by fields of late-lying snow, particularly on north-facing slopes. If these snowfields lie on steeply pitched slopes, crossing them safely may be impossible because the risk of falling is high. Turning back or taking a detour may be the only safe options.

READING THE SNOW FOR A SAFE ROUTE

Rocks underneath a blanket of snow absorb heat in the spring, causing the snow near them to melt faster than in other areas. This creates a hazard, as the soft snow may not be firm enough to hold your weight. To avoid breaking through soft snow, and perhaps injuring yourself on the rocks beneath, pick a path that avoids obvious rocky places and use trekking poles to test the snow.

BREAKING TRAIL

A climbing party walks in single file. When hiking through deep snow, take turns at the front—10–15 minutes at a time—as breaking trail (tramping down virgin snow) can be hard work.

CROSSING SUN CUPS
If crossing later in the day when the snow is soft, try to walk on the rims of sun cups. Keeping your balance can be tricky, but you are less likely to sink in.

Sun cups are depressions caused by snow melting unevenly during the day, making it very soft. They vary in size from that of a netball to a bath tub. Try to cross large snowfields early in the day, because the sun cups grow and soften as the day progresses. By late afternoon, you are likely to sink in as deep as your hips with every step.

ASCENDING ON SNOW

A mountainside trail that can be easily ascended in the dry summer months may not be safe under snow. When walking on snow, the conditions should govern your route. You may have to create your own zigzags to ascend safely, or go straight up if that is an easier option. To climb safely, kick in several times to make a solid step on which to stand with one foot. Test your weight, then climb onto the step. Now kick in again with the other foot.

ASCENDING IN DEEP SNOW

Trekking uphill through deep snow is time-consuming and exhausting. Allow at least twice as much time for this kind of hiking.

EXTRA TRACTION

Traction devices such as 12-point step-in crampons give better purchase on icy and steep terrain.

Follow in the leader's footsteps, but be prepared to take a turn at the front

Carefully test each step before moving forward

SNOW TECHNIQUES

Traveling over snow can be challenging. Techniques for descending steep or icy slopes include boot skiing, in which you slide while hopping from foot to foot to maintain balance, and glissading, when you sit and slide, usually using an ice ax for traction and braking. Snowshoeing and backcountry skiing are options for traveling in deep snow, but skiing with a heavy pack can be difficult for beginners.

SNOWSHOEING

Snowshoes spread your weight over a large area so that you walk on top of the snow instead of sinking into it. Snowshoeing is an easy technique to learn.

CROSSING FROZEN WATER

Crossing streams, lakes, and rivers requires a great deal of caution, as a thick layer of snow may cover only a thin layer of ice. When crossing ice, use your trekking poles or ice ax to probe for holes and to test the snow. You are most likely to encounter thin ice in late spring.

FINDING A SAFE ROUTE ACROSS FROZEN WATER

Do not rely on the footsteps of previous hikers to show you a safe route. Their footsteps could be one or more days old, and the route may not be safe for you if there has been an intervening warm spell.

SAFETY

FROZEN BRIDGES

Frozen snow and ice can form a bridge over a stream, which you can usually safely cross. But do not attempt to cross a bridge during the late spring snowmelt when it could collapse under your weight. Check that the snow is not dark or soft, and look for cracks. Also, test your footing before committing your weight.

GLACIER TRAVEL

Traveling on glaciers requires specialized mountaineering skills. Hidden crevasses can suddenly open underfoot, causing fatal falls. Never attempt to cross a glacier without the help of an experienced guide.

PREVENTING A FALL

The technique used for stopping a slide with an ice ax is known as "self-arrest." You should carry your ice ax in your uphill hand with the adze toward you. If you plan to travel in ice and snow, it is well worth taking a climbing class beforehand to master the technique.

SELF-ARREST TECHNIQUE

When you fall, bring the adze up to about shoulder-height. Now turn toward the adze and dig it into the snow, making sure that the ax is diagonally across your body, so the sharp point is not directly under you. Spread your weight out against the snow and dig the ax in aggressively.

Dig the ice ax in as hard as possible, and push your body into the snow

Be sure to keep crampons off the snow. Catching a point in the snow could cause you to somersault

Your face should be turned toward the snow when you dig in your ice ax

Climatic conditions

Climate is a general description of the weather patterns of a region, whereas weather refers to specific day-to-day conditions. Very few hikers truly enjoy hiking in extreme conditions such as torrential rain, scorching heat, or Arctic cold. Take time to research your destination.

Understanding weather patterns

In many regions, weather patterns are fairly predictable—prevailing winds may come from one direction, certain months of the year may be rainier than others, and storms may break at certain times of day. Finding out about characteristic local weather patterns will help you to plan your hike and ensure that you have the right gear for the conditions.

WEATHER AND GEOGRAPHY

Weather is created by the movement of air currents, the moisture content of the air, and the collision between warm and cold fronts. Weather is also affected by physical geography—by features such as mountains, large lakes, seas, and oceans.

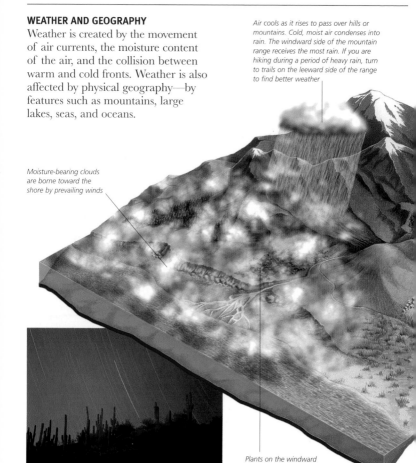

Air cools as it rises to pass over hills or mountains. Cold, moist air condenses into rain. The windward side of the mountain range receives the most rain. If you are hiking during a period of heavy rain, turn to trails on the leeward side of the range to find better weather

Moisture-bearing clouds are borne toward the shore by prevailing winds

Plants on the windward side include moisture-loving species, and they grow in more abundance than plants on the leeward side, where vegetation is sparser and water sources more sporadic

NIGHTTIME DESERT
Because there is little or no moisture in the air and no cloud cover to keep in the heat, nighttime temperatures in a desert can be much colder than in the daytime.

MOUNTAIN STORM

The mass of a mountain jutting into the sky interacts with the prevailing winds to cause storms. Electrical storms are dangerous, especially for hikers above the treeline, where there is no shelter.

The dry side of a mountain range may be very rocky, or may be covered with a thick scrub or dense vegetation through which it is difficult to hike

After depositing their rainfall on the mountains, dry winds carry little or no moisture over the leeward sides, which may vary from dry grassland to genuine desert

WEATHER PATTERNS

Nights are often clear and cold in the mountains. As the temperature increases toward morning, winds may build, and later clouds and storms form.

Despite their dry climate, deserts often have a short season of rainy weather. Desert storms can be fierce, but are usually short in duration and the rainfall is quickly absorbed or evaporated

Weather near the coast is milder than weather farther inland because of the warming effect of ocean currents. It can also be wet and cold in the winter

N
W E
S

EXTREME WEATHER

Mt. Washington is a relatively small mountain, only 6,289 ft (1,917 m) high. Its unique location at the intersection of three weather fronts, and the fact that it is the highest peak for 1,000 miles (1,600 km) in any direction, combine to create what has been called "the worst weather in the world." It also demonstrates the effect of colliding weather systems and the effect of altitude on temperature and precipitation.

Despite its elevation, Mt. Washington has the highest wind speed ever recorded on land at 231 mph (372 km/h). Hurricane-strength winds blow every three days, and the average yearly rainfall is 99 in (251 cm).

In spite of the poor weather, it is a popular hiking destination, but hikers must be well prepared for the conditions. Check with the White Mountain National Forest (www.fs.fed.us/r9/white) for current information.

MOUNT WASHINGTON

The average annual temperature recorded on the summit of Mt. Washington is only 26.5°F (–3°C). The average amount of snow that falls each year is 256 in (650 cm).

Predicting the Weather

Weather forecasting is a complicated but inexact science. A forecast that is right for a big town may not be accurate for your hiking area. You can, however, forecast the weather by observing natural signs, from the smell of the forest to the color of the sky. Many of these signs are based on scientific factors such as atmospheric pressure or moisture content of the air.

LOW AIR PRESSURE

Decreasing atmospheric pressure is a sign of bad weather. If an altimeter reading changes while you remain at the same contour, the air pressure is changing.

UNSETTLED WEATHER AHEAD
Many animals are sensitive to low air pressure. Flying insects hover closer to the ground and swallows fly low when the air pressure is dropping.

COLOR OF THE SKY

"Red sky at night, shepherd's delight" is fairly accurate if the prevailing wind direction is a westerly. It indicates the approach of fair weather.

RAIN COMING
A red sky in the morning is caused by the sun rising in the east and reflecting on high cirrus cloud, which can mean rain is on the way in the following 12 hours.

STILL AIR

A prolonged period of still air indicates an absence of atmospheric pressure changes, caused by frontal systems, that lead to unsettled weather.

CALM WEATHER
If smoke rises straight up from a fire, you can expect good weather to continue. But how long it continues will depend on regional weather patterns.

A CORONA

This ring around the moon is a sign of impending wet weather, as is a halo around the sun. Both mean bad weather is on the way in the next 12–24 hours.

WET WEATHER TO COME
Tiny ice particles in high cirrus cloud refract, bending light from the moon in a luminous ring. This moisture is a forerunner of bad weather.

READING THE CLOUDS

Clouds are formed when moisture rises into the atmosphere and condenses on small particles of dust. The movement of clouds through the sky often foretells the arrival of a moisture-bearing frontal system. Being able to recognize the common types of cloud and noting changes in their formation can help you to predict the weather.

CIRRUS AND CIRROCUMULUS CLOUDS

"Mares' tails" and "mackerel sky" are names given to high cirrocumulus and cirrus clouds that look like wispy commas, and often occur in good weather.

BAD WEATHER TO COME

When cirrus and cirrocumulus start to gather and thicken, they indicate that a front is moving in and that bad weather will arrive in 24–48 hours.

CUMULONIMBUS CLOUDS

When white puffy cumulus clouds (*below*) darken and grow vertically into cumulonimbus (anvil-shaped) clouds, rain is likely, often occuring with storms.

LIGHTNING AND THUNDER ARRIVING

Electrical charges build up in the clouds causing lightning. The resulting shock waves become the sound waves that are heard as thunder.

CUMULUS CLOUDS

Relatively thin and white, cumulus clouds look like cottonballs with flat bases. Fair-weather cumulus show only a slight vertical growth.

FAIR WEATHER

Cumulus clouds that retain their shape usually foretell a period of fair weather. These clouds often have large expanses of blue sky between them.

STRATUS CLOUDS

These long, gray, shallow clouds bring long periods of drizzly, gray weather. Made up of low layers, they often cover the whole sky, blotting out the sun.

GRAY, DRIZZLY PERIODS

The dark, low-lying stratus clouds usually foretell the least hiker-friendly weather—often meaning several days of continual rain.

Basic safety

With good planning, carefully chosen gear, solid skills, and common sense, most hikers are easily able to overcome the challenges of hiking in all kinds of terrain. Sometimes, however, the unforeseen does happen, and you need to be prepared for such eventualities.

Using instinct and judgement

The most important tool you have when out on a trail is your judgement. Deep down, you probably know what conditions you can handle and what you cannot. If you are torn between pressing on and turning back, stop to think about how you might tell the story of your misadventure in retrospect, and how you might justify the decision you are about to make.

DECIDING WHEN TO TURN AROUND

The best-laid plans are no match against nature. Storms, trail obstacles, and terrain that is more difficult than expected can all conspire to delay you or make a hike impossible to continue safely.

"Turn-back time" is a time that you set before climbing a mountain or

undertaking any sort of out-and-back hike. Decide at what point it will be necessary to turn around in order to return safely before dark, whether or not you have reached your objective.

You should always turn around when thunderstorms are rolling in, particularly if you are above the tree line, where

KNOW YOUR LIMITATIONS
In severe weather and difficult terrain, you need to evaluate whether your skills, your stamina, and your equipment are all up to the challenge.

the bare landscape offers no place to shelter. Turn around when navigation is difficult, especially when hiking cross-country, on a poorly marked trail, or in fog. You should not continue if you are exhausted, if you are shivering, or if you exhibit any other signs of hypothermia.

When you are on dangerous terrain, go back if it looks too challenging. Examples include steeply pitched ice slopes and deep rivers to ford. Consider the mountaineering motto: "Better to turn back one hundred times too early, than once too late."

HEALTH CONCERNS IN EXTREME CONDITIONS

While hiking in extreme conditions, such as high mountains or deserts where shifts of temperature happen quickly, pay attention to changes in the weather and how your body is adapting. If necessary, take appropriate action.

Sun and snow (eyes) Snow blindness is a painful sunburn of the retina. Always wear polarized and UV-filtering sunglasses when traveling above the treeline, especially when walking on snow.

Cold and rain (core) Hypothermia lowers your core temperature, causing dangerous chilling and disorientation. Hypothermia can occur in temperatures as high as 50°F (10°C), and is especially dangerous in cool rainy weather (see p.141).

Cold (fingers and toes) Your extremities are vulnerable to frostbite (see p.140).

Sun (skin) Sunburn can be a problem almost anywhere, even on cloudy days. Always wear sunscreen of SPF (sun protection factor) 15 or higher (see p.135).

Heat (throat) Dehydration causes thirst, headaches, nausea, and extreme weakness (see p.138).

Heat (blood vessels) Heat brings blood vessels to the surface, which can cause heat exhaustion or potentially fatal heatstroke (see p.139).

Heat or humidity (skin) Rashes from heat can develop where sweat is not able to escape, or where skin chafes.

Heat (feet) Feet swell and sweat in hot weather, making them more prone to blistering (see p.134).

Heat or humidity (kidney area) Hyponatremia occurs in hot weather when a hard-working body sweats out more electrolytes than it replaces, putting stress on the kidneys and other internal organs. The condition can be fatal. The best prevention is to eat small snacks regularly, and avoid dehydration.

PERSONAL SAFETY

All hikers, particularly women, should consider the following points:

■ **Whenever possible**, choose a parking area that is frequently used. Check with local trail clubs or the police whether there have been problems in the parking area. If there have, ask about alternatives in nearby towns. Some local businesses may allow you to park on their property in exchange for a fee.

■ **On the trail**, be casually friendly to hikers you meet. Do not tell others your plans or where you plan to camp.

■ **If you are hiking alone** or in a pair, and you feel uncomfortable about a person who is being overly curious or aggressive, do not be afraid to turn to fellow hikers for help. Look for a large group, tell your pursuer that you have found your friends, and wave goodbye.

■ **If sleeping** in a communal shelter, do not unpack your gear until a few other hikers have arrived and you have had time to check them out.

■ **Do not leave** expensive equipment unattended or in sight of a public road. If you are camping in a popular campsite, ask someone to keep an eye on your belongings. Alternatively, camp in a spot that is hidden from the trail.

■ **Take money** and any small, expensive gear such as cameras with you. A small lock on your tent may act as a deterrent to opportunistic thieves.

CAMPING

Sleeping in the open

Spending a night in the great outdoors can be a satisfying and peaceful part of your hiking trip. But whether you pitch a tent, rig a hammock, or sleep under the stars, be sure to follow minimum-impact guidelines and leave your sleeping area in the same condition as you found it.

Choosing a tent site

The places you choose to camp will all differ in degrees of comfort and amenities, but they should all offer some protection from the weather. Try to arrange to end your hiking day about two hours before sunset. This will allow enough time to pick a site that is both comfortable and safe, and it will give you enough time to make camp and cook before it is dark.

FINDING A SITE

The ideal tent site offers protection from wind and wind-driven rain. This protection could be a large boulder, or a small copse of shrubs and trees. Pitch your tent on the sheltered side of such windbreaks, with its back to the wind.

FINDING A BALANCE

A spectacular view makes sleeping in the open an enjoyable experience, but make sure the site you choose suits all your needs before pitching your tent.

A level site is essential for a good night's sleep, but avoid sites that have been compacted into hard depressions, as these will collect water if it rains. If you cannot avoid a slight gradient, place the head of the tent at the higher end. If you are unsure about the pitch, lie down to feel the direction of the slope.

Most hikers choose to camp near water. However, camping too close to a river can also be dangerous in seasons when flooding occurs—choose a site that is at least 100 ft (30 m) away and above any evidence of a high water line. Do not camp on a dry riverbed, because you could find yourself caught in a flash flood.

Avoid camping on obvious animal trails, especially near water sources in dry country. A tent site near a water source may frighten away animals that depend on it. Alternatively, an animal may decide to head for the water anyway, passing right through your tent site.

Your cooking area should be at least 100 ft (30 m) away from your tent, in order to keep food smells away from your sleeping area and prevent sparks from a fire (if you have one) from damaging your tent.

CAMPING NEAR WATER
If you pitch your tent near water, make sure you are far enough away to avoid the possibility of flooding or inadvertently contaminating a water source that could be used for drinking.

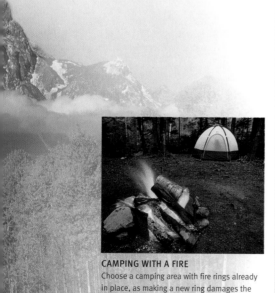

CAMPING WITH A FIRE
Choose a camping area with fire rings already in place, as making a new ring damages the environment. Pitch your tent at least 15 ft (4 m) away and upwind of a fire, to avoid cooking smells and sparks coming near your tent.

AREAS TO AVOID

Exposed, wet, or windy sites are rarely ideal for camping, but low-lying areas can also make unsuitable campsites.

TREES

Although many trees offer protection, trees with dead branches or lone trees on windswept fields, especially ones that lean at precarious angles, may be dangerous.

ROCKFALL

In high mountains, a site littered with rocks that have clearly fallen down the surrounding slopes means there is a high possibility of a rockfall.

MEADOWS

Because they are fragile environments, meadows should not be used as campsites. They may also be wet if near a river.

DRY RIVERBEDS

Riverbeds make dangerous campsites because they could be in the path of flash floods, which can occur many miles downstream of the storm that caused them.

VALLEY FLOORS

Cold air is heavier than warm air, which means that it sinks and pools on valley floors.

MOUNTAIN RIDGES

Such exposed areas are vulnerable to high winds and lightning.

MOUNTAIN PASSES

These act as wind tunnels, making them unsuitable for a tent site.

Camping with a tent

Putting up a tent is not difficult, but each one is different, and the process varies. Before going on a trip, pitch your tent in the yard (or living room) to be sure you have all the parts and know which pieces fit where. Then take it down again and stow it away. Keep the instructions for future use.

PITCHING A DOME TENT

Find an area of ground that is as flat as possible. If using a groundsheet, place it down first, to protect your tent from sharp stones. Most tents come with a built-in groundsheet; however, some of these are very lightweight. A separate groundsheet can be purchased for extra protection from damp—you can also use a piece of heavyweight plastic sheeting.

1 Clear the area of rocks or sticks that might cause discomfort or damage your tent. If using a groundsheet, lay it down. Put the elastic-corded tent poles together gently (*see inset*). Avoid snapping the sections together, as this can damage them.

2 Shake out the tent until it lies flat on the groundsheet. Carefully thread the poles through the sleeves (which may be color-coded), one at a time. Do not force the poles or you may damage the fabric. Instead, pull the fabric gently over the poles.

3 Once all the poles are in place, gently push them into their grommets. Do not put any poles into the grommets until all the poles are in place—threading a pole through the sleeve of a partially erected tent can cause it to poke through the fabric.

4 Peg the tent down. Even a freestanding tent should be pegged securely to make sure it does not blow away while you are attaching the flysheet. If the ground is too hard or rocky for pegs, tie the guy ropes around rocks or fallen trees.

TAKING DOWN A TENT

When dismantling your tent, work carefully to avoid tearing the fabric or damaging the poles.

■ Sweep away any dirt on the inside or outside of the tent. If it is a freestanding tent, shake it out after removing the tent pegs.

■ Take out the flysheet pegs. Unhook and remove the flysheet. If it is wet, shake it to remove as much of the moisture as possible.

■ Remove the pegs holding down the inner tent and disconnect the poles from the grommets.

■ Carefully remove the poles from the flysheet's sleeves in one piece (if they pull apart while in the sleeves, they will be difficult to remove).

■ Pull the pole sections apart gently, one at a time (pulling a little extra cord through each time). Fold the poles as you go.

■ Check that you have all the pegs and poles before packing up. Lay the tent flat with the flysheet on top. Fold into thirds, place the poles and pegs at one end, and roll up the tent tightly.

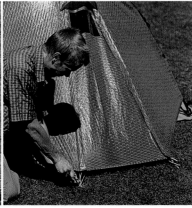

5 Put on the flysheet. First line it up with the inner tent so that it is in the correct position, then secure it with either grommets or buckles (depending on the model). The flysheet should not touch the fabric of the inner tent or moisture will penetrate.

6 Peg down the flysheet. While it is not always necessary to use all of the loops and eyelets, the more pegs you use, the more secure the tent will be. This is important in strong winds. If the tent has vents, keep them open to provide air circulation.

7 Tuck the edges of the groundsheet underneath the tent to prevent water from pooling on it, seeping into the tent, and getting your gear wet.

ERECTED TENT

The shape of this tent is created by curved poles that cross to form a self-supporting frame, making it stable and able to withstand strong winds.

UV-resistant nylon offers protection from intense sunlight in high altitudes

Camping without a tent

In fair weather, you may want the experience of sleeping out in the open, with nothing between you and the night sky. But for those who want plenty of fresh air, but also some degree of privacy and protection, there are simple shelters either available on the trail or that you can rig yourself.

USING A TRAIL SHELTER
Shelters, like the small, partly open-sided cabin shown here, are found on some trail systems. Most have hooks on which to hang your boots, backpack, and food bags to protect them from animals. The shelters are for communal use, so be prepared to make room for other hikers.

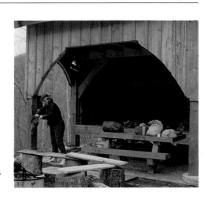

COMMUNAL SHELTER
Trail shelters usually operate on a first-come first-served basis, and can be busy at peak times. Always carry emergency shelter in case a trail shelter is full.

RIGGING A TARPAULIN
Tarpaulins are an excellent alternative in relatively dry climates where rain and insects are not a problem.

Tarpaulins are available pre-sewn, or can be made from rip-stop nylon or other waterproof, lightweight fabrics. A piece measuring 64 sq ft (6 sq m) is roomy for one hiker, and adequate for two, while 75 sq ft (7 sq m) allows plenty of space for two hikers and their gear.

Choose a large, flat area of hard-packed earth, and use adjustable trekking poles at the front and back to vary the height. Attach a length of cord at each end to keep the tarpaulin upright and stable.

In high winds, pitch one end of the tarpaulin perpendicular to the wind and pegged down at ground level. The side facing away from the wind can be higher, to give more air flow, a better view, and more headroom.

TARPAULIN SHELTER
A tarpaulin provides spacious shelter and some protection from the wind and rain, while still being open to the fresh air.

Raising one side allows air to circulate

There is plenty of room underneath for all your gear

The tarpaulin should be tightly pitched and securely pegged

SLEEPING UNDER THE STARS

Choose a comfortable, flat spot for your open-air campsite. It also needs to be somewhere dry, so avoid meadows and other areas of damp ground.

Make sure you will be warm enough, but also ensure that your sleeping bag is not too warm for the conditions. A fully zipped bag can protect you from insects, as can wearing full clothing, but if your clothes and bag are too warm, you will be uncomfortable and may be unable to sleep. Place some insect-repelling coils near your sleeping area to keep insects away.

Be sure that any items that might attract animals, such as food, are hung away from your sleeping spot (*see* pp.45 and 131). Also, do not cook or eat in close proximity to your sleeping area, as food smells can attract animals.

SLEEPING WITHOUT A SHELTER
You will not be using mosquito netting, so choose a site on slightly elevated ground, where there will be more of a breeze to blow away insects.

Be prepared for any sudden changes in the weather during the night. Have your flashlight handy and a temporary shelter that can be put up fairly quickly.

SLEEPING IN A HAMMOCK

Hammocks can be rigged up at any campsite that has trees—even if the ground is sloping, muddy, and full of rocks. Because there is no impact on the earth, a well-pitched hammock will leave very little damage. Choose a hammock with wide webbing straps that will not cut into the bark of trees (*see* p.35).

Support ropes should be of equal length at the front and back of the hammock, and tied at the same height. A tarpaulin can be suspended over the hammock if it rains at night.

In addition to using a sleeping bag, take a sleeping mat to insulate you from the cold air below the hammock, or you may become seriously chilled even on warm nights. You can make a heat-reflective sleeping mat by wrapping a foam mat in heat-reflective material, such as a metallic space blanket. A car windshield reflector can also be used as an insulator.

USING A HAMMOCK

Hammocks designed specifically for backpacking are lightweight and comfortable for all-night sleeping, and some come with an integrated flysheet.

Food and water

Proper sustenance is vital for hiking. Foresight and planning is needed if you are to make the most of opportunities to gather and replenish supplies of food and water during your trip. To enjoy hot food on the trail, you must know how to use your stove, or how to build a fire.

Staying hydrated

Water is essential to hikers. It prevents dehydration, maintains electrolyte balance, and can help prevent altitude sickness. On a short hike, you may be able to carry all the water you need. On a longer hike, you will need to find and purify enough water to keep yourself fully hydrated along the way.

WATER SOURCES

Hiking guidebooks and maps usually only contain a general guide to water sources, as conditions vary from year to year. For this reason, you should always check locally to find out the condition of water sources before setting off.

There are essentially two types of water source—surface water and spring water. Of the two, spring water is less likely to be contaminated. Surface water can be flowing or still, but a stream high in the mountains is likely to have cleaner water than a still pond or lake lower down, because it is closer to its source.

As you hike, take note of how well the water sources are running. If springs are bubbling and streams are flowing freely, you can assume that most of the water sources mentioned in your guidebook will be running. If sources appear sluggish or low, be sure to drink at every opportunity, and always carry a little more water than you think you need to reach the next reliable source. If you reach a water source that is dry, or you get lost and are unable to locate the source, you may need to use your ingenuity to find another source. (*See* pp.120–1 for how to find and distill water.)

PURIFYING WATER

There are two basic ways to treat water so that it is safe to drink. The first is to filter it—a method that removes

DESERT ENVIRONMENT

You will need to carry plenty of water in the desert. Much of the surface water in Death Valley, California, is made up of saline ponds.

SURFACE WATER
Even fast-running, clear-looking streams may be contaminated—you cannot tell just by looking. Despite the temptation to drink, take the time to purify the water first. The same applies to freezing-cold water.

microorganisms and contaminants through a filtration process. The second is purification, which kills contaminants, either with chemicals or by boiling. The major difference between the two methods is that filtering cannot remove viruses, which are too small to be trapped by a filter. While viruses are not usually a major problem in developed countries, they are a concern in less-developed parts of the world.

Water-purifying chemicals include chlorine, iodine, and potassium permanganate. Iodine tablets are the most effective and easy to use. However, it takes at least 20 minutes for iodine to kill parasites such as *Giardia lamblia* (which causes diarrhea and is common in many parts of the world), with longer times required if the water is particularly dirty.

One solution is to use a purifier equipped with both a filtration element (which catches the large cysts that iodine takes a long time to kill) and a germicidal element (such as iodine, which kills viruses that filters cannot strain). Such filters use only tiny amounts of iodine compared to iodine tablets, making this a faster and more efficient method of water filtration.

MELTING SNOW

In the winter, or at higher elevations, you have an unlimited supply of water in frozen form.

■ **Do not try to** quench your thirst by eating snow —it will simply reduce your body temperature without providing enough moisture to satisfy your thirst. Always melt it first.

■ **Choose an area** with a large supply of clean-looking snow, avoiding snow heavily marked with animal tracks.

■ **Gather snow** in clean, black garbage bags (which absorb heat), and leave them in the sun to melt. For quicker results, use your stove and pots.

■ **Light the stove** and heat at least a cupful of water. (If you try to melt snow directly in a hot pan, the pan will scorch.)

■ **Add the snow** slowly, one cup at a time, waiting until each cup has melted before adding more.

■ **Remove the water** from the pan and pour it into a dark fabric water bag.

■ **Place this bag** in the sun, where the dark color will absorb heat and warm the water to a comfortable drinking temperature.

WATER CONSUMPTION

The amount of water you need to drink depends on your body size, the temperature, the altitude, and the amount you are exercising. When you set out, carry at least one liter of water for one hour's hiking in cool weather. Carry more if it is hotter, you are overweight, or water resources are scarce. Use the chart below as a guide.

SEASON	ESTIMATE PER DAY (MAX)	ACTUAL CONSUMPTION PER HOUR
SUMMER	15 PINTS	2 PINTS
WINTER	9 PINTS	1 – 2 PINTS

Add snow slowly

Water heated in pan

HOW TO MELT SNOW

Restocking food supplies

Whenever possible, choose foods that resist spoilage, are easy to pack, and are lightweight. However, once the supplies you brought with you have run out, you may have to restock in small towns where there is little choice. It is important to choose wisely and cook hygienically to avoid illness.

STAPLE HIKING FOODS

The basic food items in a hiking diet—rice, pasta, and varieties of grain—can be bought in most places, and so are easy to restock. These dry foods are lightweight because they contain no water, and are less subject to spoilage. Dried potatoes are a popular staple, and can be eaten mixed with a variety of foods. Choose quick-cook versions.

FOODS TO AVOID

Keep away from overly fatty foods, especially dairy food and meats, which can become rancid and spoil in hot weather. Though delicious and tempting, restrict your intake of fruit to avoid developing diarrhea. Avoid lettuce because it is easily contaminated by unhygienic growing methods or washing in contaminated water.

SAFE AND EASY TRAVEL FOODS

FOOD STAPLES

Nonperishable foods are safe choices that will keep for the duration of your trip, providing that you keep them in dry, sealed containers. Choose foods that cook quickly to save fuel. In cool climates, certain perishable foods can be kept for several days in ziplocked bags (with the air excluded). Pack them in the center of your bag for extra insulation.

NONPERISHABLE		PERISHABLE	
	Rice Instant rice is less nutritious than standard rice, but it cooks quickly, saving fuel		**Salami** Hard salami lasts well, even in hot weather
	Cereals Choose instant hot cereal, or simply add hot water and dried milk to a cold cereal		**Sausages** Dried, spiced sausages last longer than soft varieties
	Sardines Tinned sardines last indefinitely. Choose cans with built-in openers		**Cheeses** Hard cheeses last longer than soft cheeses

THE NO-COOK CAMPSITE

Some hikers find that for short trips in hot weather, it is more convenient to travel without a stove and to eat only cold food. This saves the weight of cooking gear, but foods that can be eaten cold, without adding water, are generally heavier than their counterparts that need to be cooked. This strategy therefore works only for shorter trips.

- Dried fruits
- Dried meats
- Nuts
- Peanut butter
- Cheeses
- Yeast-extract spread
- Canned meats and fish
- Canned beans
- Just-add-cold-water food mixes
- Fresh fruit
- Wholegrain breads
- Crackers
- Cereal bars
- Raw vegetables (such as carrots, cabbage, cauliflower, broccoli, celery)

Finding food in the wild

For most hikers, wild foods are an interesting experiment, but not a reliable source of nourishment. Finding edible wild foods requires knowledge of their habitat, and being able to identify them is vital. If you do gather food in the wild, be sure not to overharvest any one area.

EDIBLE PLANTS

A host of familiar berries grow in fields and forests during the summer. Gather berries in a water bottle and use them to flavor breakfast cereals (never eat white berries—almost all of them are poisonous).

Many plants are entirely or partially edible. Chives (a wild member of the onion family) can be used to flavor sauces, while the leaves of dandelions can be eaten as salad leaves.

Wash all wild foods with clean water before eating them. As a rule, do not eat anything that you cannot positively identify as safe to eat. Remember that some plants are edible only at certain stages of their growth.

KNOW YOUR WILD FOOD

If you plan to eat wild plants, memorize their distinguishing features and habitats, along with any poisonous lookalikes for which they could be mistaken.

Edible berries are sweet, juicy, and rich in vitamins

BLUEBERRIES

Highly flavored, fleshy leaves

Wash berries with clean water before eating them

BILBERRIES

Most white berries are poisonous, so should never be eaten

WHITE BERRIES

WILD CHIVES

Leaves give a bitter taste to salads

Umbrella-shaped clusters identify the flower

The root is best eaten when young

DANDELION LEAF

WILD CARROT ROOT AND FLOWERS

FISHING FOR FOOD

If you want to dine on fresh fish, plan your hiking days so that you can cast your line when the fish are biting. You may also find mussels or other shellfish along the coast. Before catching fish or shellfish, be sure you have any necessary licenses or permits, and check that local fish and shellfish are safe to eat (the waters may be contaminated).

SAFETY

You are more likely to become sick from unhygienic eating and cooking practices than from contaminated water.

■ Wash hands before handling food, cooking, and eating.

■ Do not share utensils and dishes.

■ Bring any water to be used in cooking to a rolling boil first. If you add cold water to a soup or stew, make sure the meal returns to the boil for at least a minute before serving.

■ Wash dishes in bottled, boiled, or purified water.

■ Clean dishes and pots with biodegradable soap and a small scouring pad, or use sand or gravel to remove food particles.

■ Periodically scour the threads of your water bottles, and rinse with treated water.

Using a stove

A portable hiking stove takes only a few minutes to be primed, lit, and ready to cook, making it much quicker than building and lighting a fire. But stoves need to be used properly in order to work efficiently. Before you set off, test a new stove at home to be sure you understand how it works. If you do this, you will be able to start cooking a meal very quickly.

INCREASING STOVE EFFICIENCY

A few simple techniques can reduce cooking time and hence the amount of fuel you need to carry. Always use a pot lid to keep in heat—some stove sets have pot lids that can be used as frying-pans.

Lids can also be used as warmers for sauces while you cook pasta or grains inside the pot. You can also trap heat with a heat reflector or a windscreen. A heat exchanger, which attaches directly to the pot, is also very effective.

Aluminum sheet shields the flame from wind

Heat from burner is held close to the pot

Heat under the pot is reflected back up

Folds out to fit under legs of cooking unit

The amount of fuel used is reduced

WINDSCREEN
To shield the stove flame from the wind, these are essential on a blustery day. Some windscreens come with a stove, but you can buy them separately.

HEAT REFLECTORS
A circular piece of aluminum placed under the burner will reflect heat back up toward the cooking pot. Heat reflectors weigh little and stow away easily.

USING A CANISTER STOVE

Make sure you buy the correct type of canister for your stove. Fix the stove to the canister and then light it. Some are self-igniting, but always carry dry matches, because flint can wear out.

1 Place the stove on a firm surface in a well-ventilated area. Turn the knob on the side that releases the fuel from the canister to the burner.

2 Holding the canister steady with your hand, flick the self-igniting flint. The flame should catch and light the fuel immediately. Adjust the flame.

USING A LIQUID FUEL STOVE

Different types of liquid fuel stoves vary slightly, but the simple mechanics of this popular model are common to many of them. Fuel flows from the container to the burner, where it is ignited to produce a steady flame.

1 Pump the fuel pump to pressurize the fuel bottle. About 20 strong strokes should result in resistance—this indicates that the fuel bottle is pressurized. If the fuel bottle is not full, you will need to pump more strokes.

2 Open the fuel control valve 1–2 turns to release the liquid fuel, and allow it to half fill the priming cup. Turn off the fuel valve. You should be able to see liquid fuel pooling in the priming cup. (Check for leaks at this stage.)

Priming cup

3 Light the liquid gas with a match or lighter. It may flare quite high. Wait for the flame to lower and start burning more strongly—the flame will be blue, and you will hear the distinctive roaring sound of combustion.

4 Open the fuel valve to let more fuel come through. The flame should settle into a steady, low roar. If the combustion seems uneven, try repressurizing the fuel pump with a few more strokes (*see* step 1).

COOKING ESSENTIALS

For stoves that do not self-ignite, you need a lighter or matches, both of which need to be reliable in wet weather.
■ Carry windproof, waterproof matches.
■ If you use standard matches, dip the tips in paraffin or wax to make them waterproof. Scrape off the wax before lighting.
■ If your matches are wet, in an emergency, you can use a magnifying glass to focus sunlight on the tinder to light a fire. Many compasses contain magnifying glass.

STOVE SAFETY

Portable stoves are safe to use if handled carefully. The following steps will ensure safe operation:
■ **Inspect your stove** before taking it on a trip, and always use, maintain, and clean the stove according to the manufacturer's instructions.
■ **Never cook inside** a tent. Risks include flare-ups (flames out of control), fire, and asphyxiation from carbon monoxide fumes.
■ **Always set the stove** securely on a firm surface before putting a pot on top of it. Do not use an over-sized pot—a 3½ pt (2 liter) pot is about the maximum size that can be safely used on most small camp stoves.
■ **Use only the type** of fuel recommended for your stove.
■ **Be sure to mark** your fuel bottle so that it cannot be confused with a water bottle.
■ **Make sure your** fuel bottle does not leak.
■ **Do not fill** a liquid fuel bottle to the top. Liquid fuel stoves burn fuel more efficiently when the bottles are about three-quarters full, because when the pump is pressurized, the air in the container puts pressure on the fuel and helps it to flow smoothly.
■ **Flare-ups** and incomplete combustion (evident by an orange rather than a blue flame) are signs of malfunction.
■ **Wait until a hot** stove cools before you relight it.
■ **Wait for a hot stove** to cool before you clean it.

Making a fire

The advent of portable stoves means that fewer hikers use fires for cooking. Indeed, in some ecologically fragile or heavily used areas, fires may not be permitted. But a fire can still be an invaluable source of heat and a method of signaling. The ability to build and light a fire is essential.

BUILDING A FIRE

A successful fire needs plenty of dry material, from tiny pieces of tinder to thick sticks and even small branches. Gather your wood first and organize it into piles according to size. Resist the temptation to load too much fuel on the fire too quickly—add sticks gradually.

1 Never make a new fire-ring if you can use an existing one. However, if you must make a fire in a new place, first clear the ground of flammable debris. If making a fire in a grassy area, use a-knife to cut out turf about 1 ft (30 cm) in diameter, and set it aside to replace when you have finished. Surround the fire area with a ring of stones and build a small pile of tinder.

2 Over the tinder pile, build a small teepee using sticks about the size of a pencil. Start with a couple of forked sticks, which will balance more easily against each other and provide a stable frame on which to lean others to form the shape. The advantage of this construction is that if the sticks are slightly wet, the heat from the burning tinder will dry them before they catch light.

3 Around the outside of the teepee, place three medium-sized stones (about the size of a grapefruit). These can be used to support your pot. Never use stones from a riverbed, as they may have absorbed water and could explode when they are heated. If you have extra tinder or flammable material such as bark or pine needles, sprinkle a little more around the teepee.

FUEL TYPES

Tinder is the smallest building block of your fire and can be any small material that ignites quickly—bark, pine needles, dry twigs, moss, grass, and paper are ideal. These will burn long enough to light other larger pieces of fuel. Kindling is small bits of wood and tiny twigs that will ignite easily. Small twigs no bigger than a pencil should be used to form the foundation of your teepee. Logs and branches will provide sustaining heat.

TINDER   KINDLING   TWIGS   BRANCHES

FIRELIGHTERS

In addition to windproof, waterproof matches and a lighter, carry a small amount of material that ignites very quickly and burns long enough to help a sluggish fire get going.

- Crumpled-up pages of an old guidebook
- Waxed milk cartons, cut into slivers
- Birthday candles
- Paraffin firelighters
- Homemade balls of sawdust and wax
- Lint from the pockets of your clothing
- A cotton swab coated with petroleum jelly

LIGHTING TIPS

Fires can be difficult to make in high winds, or after long periods of rain.
- Choose a site protected from the wind.
- Look for dry wood inside hollow tree stumps, or close to the trunks of trees.
- Whittle away wet bark to find dry wood, which can be shaved into tinder.
- Gather more tinder than you think you will need.

4 Add more sticks to the teepee, building it up gradually. Ideally, the largest stick should be no thicker than your thumb, and no more than about 1 ft (30 cm) long. Leave a space at one side, so that you can reach inside the teepee to add more tinder if necessary.

5 Reach into the teepee and light the tinder. Once the tinder is burning, add pieces of fuel such as kindling and twigs, one piece at a time. When the heat builds up so that the teepee collapses, place the pot on the stones over the burning embers and start cooking.

USING A FIRE RING

Try to use existing fire rings. Fire rings help to contain the fire, but too many rings in popular areas has an unsightly visual impact.

Stones are stacked in a ring around the fire area to protect the surrounding ground

FIRE SAFETY

Forest fires are sometimes caused by camp fires that burn out of control.
- Dry, windy conditions are extremely dangerous. A fire should only be made in such conditions in an emergency. Build the fire on the leeward side (the side sheltered from the wind) of a rock wall, and keep it as small as possible.
- Build the fire on dirt, sand, or gravel and clear the area of flammable material, such as pine needles and twigs.
- Overhanging trees can accidentally catch fire from errant sparks.
- Keep fires small—pieces of wood should be no larger than your forearm.
- Sparks from some types of wood can fly long distances. Keep your fire at a safe distance from tents and sleeping bags.
- Keep a pan of water near the fire at all times, and never leave a fire unattended.
- When you have finished with the fire, extinguish it thoroughly by covering with sand, dirt, and water.

No-trace camping

As hiking has become more popular worldwide, it has had an impact on the environment. In some cases, the landscape has been scarred from overuse, and water sources have been contaminated. Some common-sense precautions can help ensure that your stay leaves no trace.

Using no-trace techniques

The basic concept of "leave no trace" is quite simple—leave things as pristine as you found them, if not a little better. Areas of particular concern are sanitation, hygiene, and campsite degradation. Overuse of fires is also damaging, especially in regions where wood is very scarce.

BEING ENVIRONMENTALLY CONSCIOUS
In order to make the least impact on the environment, read about your destination in advance. Find out which times of year attract the most tourists, and consider whether hiking in a nearby area would offer the same terrain and a similar experience without the crowds. Visit in a small group, so that you have a minimal impact on the environment. When walking, stay on the trail—in particular, do not cut switchbacks, as this leads to erosion. On marshy or boggy ground, try to stay in the middle of the trail, rather than edging around it, because this can cause the trail to widen into an unsightly bog. Always pitch your tent on a firm, stable surface.

Find out what the regulations are, especially rules about permits and fires. Always obey campfire regulations, use stoves rather than campfires to cook on, and avoid making fires in fragile regions

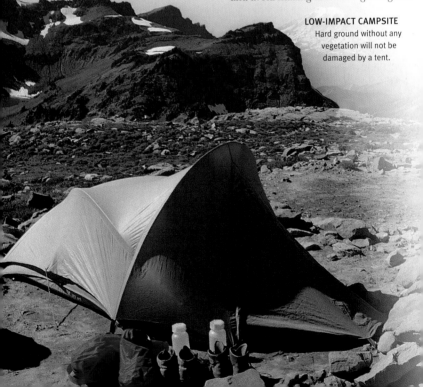

LOW-IMPACT CAMPSITE
Hard ground without any vegetation will not be damaged by a tent.

STICKING TO MARKED PATHS
In very popular areas, such as the Lake District in the UK, large numbers of tourists have a huge impact on the landscape. Keep to public footpaths across farmland and do not take shortcuts.

such as deserts and alpine tundra. Do not make fires in arid climates when high winds are blowing. Take away everything that you have brought in, including all your garbage—any hidden garbage will be found by animals and may be scattered around the area.

Avoid bringing home cultural souvenirs such as ancient arrowheads, pottery shards, or other items you might find. Such archaeological remains should be left for others to enjoy or study. The remote area you are visiting is home to a community of animals, so avoid camping on game trails, or close to water sources used by them (especially in an arid area). Never feed wild animals because those that depend on human food can become dangerous or destructive pests at campsites. They can also be made sick by an unnatural diet or even starve once the visitor season is over.

LOCAL CUSTOMS AND ETIQUETTE
In foreign countries, try to learn enough about local customs and etiquette to avoid giving inadvertent offense, especially at religious sites. When hiking across private property, respect landowners, stay on trails, and leave gates as you found them. Be aware of your impact—both visual and aural—on other hikers, and follow the no trace adage: "Take only photographs, leave only footprints."

CLEANING UP A CAMPSITE

Areas that are popular with campers can deteriorate. Try to leave each site cleaner than you found it and carry out all your litter. If you made a fire ring, replace the grass sod and restore the area to its original condition. If you used an existing fire ring, clean out any garbage, be sure no food remains on the ground, and leave the area around the fire ring tidy.

HIKING ESSENTIALS

KEEPING WATER CLEAN

Keeping yourself clean without polluting the environment can be a challenge on a long hike.
■ Use biodegradable soap.
■ Take advantage of natural baths—streams and lakes—but do not bathe in springs from which others will draw water. Try not to swallow any water, just in case it is contaminated.
■ When using soap, carry water away from the source in a container and use it to wash, so that soap does not enter the source. Scatter used wash water over a large area for minimal impact.

LATRINES AND SANITATION

A few simple procedures can help to preserve an area's cleanliness.
■ When traveling in small groups, each member of the party should dig a small hole about 6 in (15 cm) deep with their toilet trowel. The hole can be re-covered with dirt once it has been used. Site the hole at least 295 ft (90 m) from any water source.
■ Larger groups can share a latrine. Dig a deep pit out of view, at least 295 ft (90 m) from a water source, and downwind from the tents. Screen it with some vegetation to provide privacy. Scatter earth into it after each use to avoid bad smells, which attract flies.
■ Soiled personal hygiene products should be stored in sealed ziplocking bags and taken away when you leave, or burned on site.

OVERCOMING CHALLENGES

Improvizing in the field

How you choose to respond to situations you encounter in the field is a matter of flexibility and skill—the ability to apply your knowledge and your equipment to the unexpected. And as you gain experience, you will also acquire the confidence you need to be able to cope.

Spending the night outside

A sudden violent storm, illness, injury, or the rare event of being so thoroughly lost that you cannot find your way back to the start of the trail, are just a few reasons why you may need to spend an unexpected night outside. Knowing how to find or improvize a quick, secure shelter means that you will have a safe place to spend the night while waiting for help or daylight. If you are injured and cannot walk, you may need to signal for help.

USING NATURAL FEATURES

The simplest way to spend a night in the open is to lay your sleeping bag and mat in a dry, sheltered spot. If you are on an open hillside, descend. Look for trees or large rocks or a wall of stones (a "redoubt") to break the wind. Look out too for trail shelters and shepherd's huts.

SHELTERING UNDER A TREE
Evergreen trees give the best protection from the rain. Look for thick groves of evergreens but make sure your sleeping bag is protected from wet ground.

MAKING AN EMERGENCY LEAN-TO

You can construct an emergency lean-to using pieces of dead wood and foliage. If possible, use a large fallen log as the main structural component of your shelter. Lean large branches and sticks against the log to form a lean-to under which you can crawl. Cover these large sticks with a layer of branches that have leaves, interweaving the branches among the sticks, or holding them in place with twine or rope. The thicker the layer of leaves, the more the protection offered. Build the lean-to in a sheltered area because it will have little integral strength against the force of the wind.

Emergency gear such as garbage bags and space blankets can be draped over your lean-to to add extra protection. Any discarded materials you find, such as pieces of cardboard, plastic sheeting, or corrugated iron, can also be used. Wear your rain jacket to retain heat and keep water away from your clothes.

A large fallen log supports the lean-to

Long branches and sticks propped against the log form the roof

CONSTRUCTING A LEAN-TO
An emergency lean-to may not be luxurious but it can provide effective shelter.

Layers of small, leafy branches, interweaved among the larger branches, keep out wind and rain

MAKING A SNOW SHELTER

In an emergency, time and energy are in short supply and conditions are, by definition, difficult, so it is practical to choose a simple design for a shelter. To shelter from the wind, first make snow bricks and form them into a wall. This wall can be used in conjunction with a tent or as part of an emergency shelter. To make a shelter, pitch a tarpaulin or a space blanket to the lee side of the wall, and secure it in place with a layer of snow. Body heat is lost through contact with the ground, so in any snow shelter, be sure to place as much insulation (clothing, stuff sacks, a garbage bag, a backpack, sticks, branches from evergreen trees—anything you have or can find) between your body and the ground. Here are some other types of snow shelter:

MAKE A ROOFED TRENCH

Dig a trench in the snow, then use a blanket or garbage bag to form a roof (be sure to make an air hole). This can be used on a clear night, but should not be used if snow is falling because the roof could collapse.

Space blanket stretched across trench forms roof

Insulating layers help reduce loss of body heat

Hold roof in place with heavy rocks or gear

USE A TREE HOLLOW

A natural hollow is often found under a tree, especially a large conifer. Lower branches overhanging the hollow may form a kind of roof to block out wind and snow, which makes this a good natural shelter.

Low leafy branches form roof

Hollow beneath tree provides shelter

DIG A SNOW CAVE

A snow cave can be dug into the side of a large snowdrift. Make an entry hole at the low side of the drift, and dig up from the entrance to carve out a sleeping shelf. Block the entry hole behind you with snow. Poke ventilation holes in the ceiling to provide plenty of fresh air. This will also stop snow from the roof dripping on you as the air that you breathe out causes it to melt.

Ventilation hole in ceiling provides fresh air

Use a trekking pole to keep the air hole open in case of snowfall

Sleeping shelf carved out of snowdrift

Once inside snow cave, block entry hole with snow

SIGNALING FOR HELP

Ensure that there is a clear line of sight from your signal to any rescuers. Try to mark the way to your shelter with a trail of brightly colored gear.

LIGHT A FIRE

Smoke from a fire is highly visible if lit in an open area. Put damp wood or vegetation on the fire to increase the smoke.

USE A MIRROR

Point the mirror toward the sun, then move it back and forth so that the light it reflects can be seen from different vantage points. If an aircraft is within range, catch the light on the mirror, angled toward the plane.

DISPLAY ORANGE GEAR

The color orange and number three are both signs for help. Pile orange gear together in a visible place, or make three highly visible piles.

MAKE GROUND SYMBOLS

Make outlines on the ground, using brightly colored gear, branches, or rocks. Symbols that are internationally recognized by pilots are: "I" to indicate a serious injury; "F" means you need food and water.

SOUND WHISTLE BLASTS

Signal SOS with three short blasts, three long, then three short. Repeat this frequently.

Finding water

A ready supply of fresh drinking water is essential for your health—indeed, for your survival. Always check on the reliability and cleanliness of water sources before hiking in a new area.

When hiking, you should drink freely at every opportunity, even if you are not thirsty. Carry a little more water than you think you will need, so there is no danger of running short.

CARRYING WATER

Water weighs 1 lb per pint (1 kg per liter). How much you need will depend on the weather and terrain, but 1¾ pt (1 liter) is only sufficient for a day hike of an hour or two, making it impractical, if not impossible, to carry enough for a longer hike. This means that you must find water sources along your route. Note that any water you find should be purified before you drink it.

NATURAL WATER SOURCES

Seasonal waterways will be lined with vegetation, and the thicker and greener it is, the better the chance of finding water. In arid country, a strip of green running along a depression generally indicates a seasonal watercourse. Willows and cottonwoods are thirsty plants that need a fairly reliable supply, so a large grove of cottonwoods is almost always a sure sign of water. Digging in the cool sand or soil under willows can also sometimes yield water.

If you find a seasonal source that is dry, do not assume that it will be dry throughout its course. Walk downstream a little to see if the vegetation appears more lush. Look for puddles and search under large rocks, which provide shade and delay evaporation. If the ground looks as though it has recently been wet, try digging—you may find water just an inch or so below the surface.

Water can be found in shaded rock crevices, especially if they are on the north side of a hill, and springs are often marked on maps. Animals also depend on water, so look for animal tracks—in a dry country, they may lead to a source.

MANMADE WATER SOURCES

In addition to signs of natural sources, you can look for evidence of structures such as wells or water mills. Humans cannot survive in settlements without a water source, so a cluster of buildings shown on a map may indicate a source, even if the area is currently uninhabited. Note, however, that wells found in a deserted settlement may be capped or broken. There is also the possibility that the source has become polluted.

FINDING A SOURCE

Lush vegetation is a good indicator of water in dry regions. Trees such as cottonwoods, willows, and alders need plenty of water and generally grow close to perennial sources.

DISTILLING WATER

This method of obtaining water using a still (a device for distilling) is based on two scientific facts. First, a plant transpires (gives off water vapor) through its leaves. Second, the difference in temperature between two surfaces causes water vapor to condense.

1 Dig a deep hole that is wider than your container. Choose soft sandy ground, if possible. For digging in harder ground, use a toilet trowel to loosen the soil.

2 When the hole is deep enough—2 ft (60 cm) is ideal—sit a suitable container at the bottom. You can use a cup, bowl, or plastic container.

3 Surround the container with vegetation. The more dense you make the layer of vegetation (and the bigger the hole), the more effective your still will be and the more water it will yield.

4 Cover the hole with a piece of plastic and weigh it down around its edges with rocks. Put a small rock in the center to indent the plastic and act as a funnel on the underside of the plastic.

HOW A STILL WORKS

A simple solar still such as this produces water using vegetation, the sun's rays, and simple physics.

The condensed water vapor runs down the underside of the plastic and drips into the container beneath

Water vapor from the vegetation condenses on the underside of the plastic

COLLECTING TIPS

USE A WIDE-MOUTHED BOTTLE

A wide-mouthed bottle can be used to collect water from all kinds of sources, including shallow pools and streams.

USE A NATURAL CONTAINER

Large leaves and tubes from hollow grasses such as bamboo can be used to collect and funnel water from small springs. This takes some patience, but allows you to collect water from a slow source.

USE A HANDKERCHIEF

If the water source is so shallow that you simply cannot use a bottle, spread a clean handkerchief on the surface (to avoid stirring up dirt). When it has absorbed as much as possible, wring it out into your cup.

COLLECT RAINWATER

Lay out a waterproof tarpaulin, garbage bag, or groundsheet on a sloping piece of land, and fix it tightly in place with tent pegs. Place a rock in the middle to help funnel the water to the center of the material so it can flow downhill into a waiting container.

FIND PLANT SOURCES

Some cacti can provide liquid. The leaves of the prickly pear can be chewed (remove the thorns first), while the pulp of a barrel cactus can be mashed to produce a liquid. Be sure you can identify these, as other varieties can be toxic.

Severe weather

The best advice regarding severe weather is to avoid it. Of course, this may not always be possible, especially if you have traveled a long distance to your destination, or if you are on a long hike in high mountains or other regions where the weather is unpredictable.

Hiking in storms and heat

While prolonged periods of bad weather can spoil the enjoyment of a hike, several strategies can help you prevent the trip from becoming a disaster. Torrential rain may soak you, lightning may scare you, a heat wave may bake you, and humidity may sap your energy. But knowing how best to shelter from or cope with the elements will ensure your safety.

TORRENTIAL RAIN

If you are hiking in a region where heavy rain falls in short showers, you can dry out your gear during dry or sunny periods. However, in some regions, you can expect long periods of heavy rain. Guidebooks and local land management agencies will tell you whether your chosen hiking area is prone to unpredictable storms or sustained rain. Be aware that one side of a mountain range can be very wet while another is quite dry. Always be prepared to detour to a different trail in search of drier conditions.

Rainstorms in high mountains may cause flash floods that take hikers by surprise. The floods typically follow dry streambeds, which can quickly become raging torrents. For this reason, never camp in a dry streambed, even if the sky is clear and rain is not predicted. Choose a campsite on higher ground.

LIGHTNING, TORNADOES, AND HURRICANES

It is dangerous to be in a lightning storm on a mountain above the treeline where there is no shelter. Act immediately and descend as quickly as you can, looking for cover. A grove of trees is the best natural shelter—the thicker the tree cover, the greater the level of protection. Do not stand under a solitary tree, as it can act as a lightning conductor. Never shelter in a shallow cave, on a ledge, or in a depression, since these can all attract ground lightning. Finally, avoid wet areas, which also attract lightning. Sit on your pack to insulate yourself from wet ground.

If no shelter is in sight and the lightning is dangerously near, crouch down as low to the ground as you can, while minimizing your contact with the earth. Use your arms to shield your head.

Tornadoes and hurricanes are seasonal events and rarely arrive unannounced. A small radio enables you to get up-to-date forecasts. Radio stations report "tornado

SHELTERING FROM A STORM
Dense, low tree foliage provides safe natural shelter from rain and lightning.

watches" (when the conditions are right for a tornado) and "tornado warnings" (when a tornado has been spotted). As soon as you hear a tornado warning, leave the area. If you cannot escape, seek shelter in a cave or ravine, or—as a last resort—a ditch. Hurricanes form at sea and may travel great distances before reaching land, so you usually have several days' warning. During this time, you can decide upon a route back to shelter.

HEAT WAVES

Intense heat can cause exhaustion, dehydration, and heatstroke (see pp.138–9), particularly in dry places or on tough trails with steep climbs. Slow your walking pace and take breaks whenever possible, especially in the middle of the day. Put on a light-colored, reflective or vented hat that allows air to circulate: this protects your head, and helps to keep bugs away. Avoid sunburn by wearing protective loose-fitting, well-ventilated clothes that cover your arms and legs, and by regularly applying a high-factor sunscreen.

Your water requirement will increase to 5 pints (3 liters) or more a day. Take frequent, small sips, and never walk past a water source without having a drink and filling your bottle. If you find a fresh lake or stream, take the chance to bathe in it. This gives instant relief from the heat and also removes sweat from your skin, helping to prevent heat rashes. Pay attention to your feet. Feet sweat and swell in hot weather, making them larger, wetter, and more prone to blistering.

SEVERE HUMIDITY

Humidity is common in hot climates, but may also occur in temperate regions in the summer. It is more comfortable to walk in sparsely forested uplands where the air is drier and cooler than in low-lying forests. Choose a trail that includes rest places or destinations near waterfalls, lakes, or streams. Wear wicking, ventilated

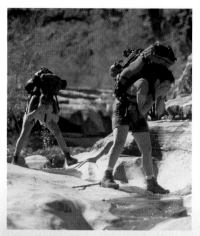

COOLING OFF
In sweltering weather, a few minutes at a cold pool of water can refresh your body, and your spirits.

clothing to avoid heat rashes and wash yourself and your clothing frequently to avoid a build-up of sweat. Drink regularly and eat easily digestible snacks to replenish the salts and sugars you are losing through sweat and exertion.

HOW TO SURVIVE A FOREST FIRE

Leave the area if you can, and go as far away from the fire as possible. If you cannot leave, look for the safest place to shelter.

■ If there is a natural fire break, such as a road or river, cross to the other side of it.

■ Look for a vegetation-free zone, such as a rock field or lake. The larger the area, the less smoke you will have to inhale.

■ Never descend into a valley where a fire is burning—the more ridges between you and the fire, the safer you are.

■ After the fire, watch out for burning, overhanging branches and ground fires, which can flare up suddenly.

■ If you are in a flammable area, lie face down on the barest patch of ground and cover yourself with soil. Put your mouth against the soil and breathe through it.

Lie face down and breathe through the soil

FOREST FIRE SURVIVAL

Hiking in fog, snow, and extreme cold

Fog, snow, and extreme cold are not conditions reserved for winter hikers. In many high mountain ranges, a summer's day can produce four seasons' worth of weather. Hikers should be prepared for cold and wet conditions, and should be particularly on guard against hypothermia.

BANKS OF FOG

Fog usually occurs in unsettled weather, and it is a particular problem in high mountains, on moorland, and along some coastlines. A bank of fog can roll in very quickly—more quickly than a hiker can move—and can be particularly dangerous when traveling cross-country as it obscures the landscape. You will not be able to see landmarks that would normally help to orientate you, making map reading difficult and using a compass impossible. Navigation will be much easier if you use a GPS receiver, which gives you an exact position.

Inside a bank of fog, it is cold, wet, and often windy. If you see a fog bank rolling toward you, add a warm layer and put on a waterproof jacket and pants right away. If you need to stop frequently to navigate, you may have to add more layers. In a group, stay in close contact, ensuring that you are always within calling distance of other people. It is a good idea to use a whistle—the sound carries further than a shout.

UNEXPECTED SNOWFALL

Mountain weather is unpredictable and snow storms can occur at any time of the year in most of the world's highest mountain ranges, even at the height of summer. Such snow may fall in brief flurries or for more prolonged periods, covering trails. Your progress may be slowed down, but summer snows usually melt quite quickly, so you will have time to catch up on your schedule.

Summer trails are not usually designed with snow in mind, and even a thin layer of snow can make traversing rocky, uneven terrain hazardous—use trekking poles for balance if you need to.

Route-finding can be difficult when the trail is covered in snow. It may be easier to navigate to the next visible destination rather than trying to follow a trail buried under snow.

LOW VISIBILITY

Even in summer, sudden fog can obscure the trail, making navigation difficult. If the fog is thick, you may have to wait for it to clear before continuing.

Fifty percent of body heat is lost through the head. A hat will prevent much of this heat from escaping

Wear socks over gloves for an extra layer of warmth for hands

Drink a cup of hot, instant soup to reduce the chills

SURVIVING THE COLD
Staying dry and warm is vital. Wear wicking layers to remove sweat from your body, protect your extremities, and change out of any wet clothing.

EXTREME COLD
Sudden, extreme cold is always a possibility in mountainous areas. In the summer, there is an increased likelihood that cold weather will be accompanied by rain. This is a dangerous combination that can lead to hypothermia (*see* p.141), so it is important to stay dry. If you do get wet, it is vital to warm up quickly.

AVOIDING AVALANCHE DANGER

Avalanches are most likely to occur in the winter, but hikers in high mountains in late spring may encounter them, too. They are most common on sunward slopes (south-facing in the northern hemisphere, north-facing in the southern hemisphere) and on the leeward side of a ridge. Avalanches tend to follow the same paths year after year, so slopes with sheared-off trees are a sure sign of danger, as is a clear chute below a cornice. Most avalanches occur on slopes with an angle of 30–45 degrees, and they are most likely in the 24 hours after a heavy snowfall.

■ **In avalanche conditions,** carry an avalanche beacon, avalanche probes (which can be trekking poles), and a shovel.

■ **Cross avalanche slopes** in the early morning. The risk of avalanche increases as the temperature rises during the day.

■ **Step cautiously and check** that the snow is solid. Avalanches can be set off by loud noises or the pressure of a person's steps, so move carefully. If you are in a group, cross the slope one at a time.

■ **Unbuckle your pack belt** before crossing the slope, so that you can drop your pack easily in case of an avalanche. Loosen hiking-pole straps, and zip up clothing (to keep out the snow). If you have a GPS receiver, set it to the "transmit" position.

■ **If you see an avalanche** coming, attempt to run downhill and away from it.

■ **If you become trapped** under snow, move your hands in front of your face to clear an air hole. Push a pole or stick upward through the snow so that rescuers can find you.

HEAD FOR THE SURFACE
If an avalanche knocks you down, lie on your front and try to "swim" your way toward the surface and out of the snow.

Getting back on route

Being lost eventually happens to many hikers who venture off well-worn trails. It can also happen on marked trails in foggy weather, in snow, if trails are only sporadically marked, or if you simply take a wrong turn. Often, reviewing your trip reveals where you are.

Using a map to find your way

Becoming lost happens slowly, over a period of time. Realizing you are lost happens very suddenly. Because it is so unexpected, you may feel disorientated. To remedy the situation, you need to work out where you deviated from your route, how long ago, and how to get back to the trail.

LOCATING YOUR POSITION

To work out where you should go, you first need to find out where you are now. Comfort yourself with the fact that, since you have probably been traveling at no more than 2–3 miles (3–5 km) per hour, it is unlikely that you are as lost as you fear you might be. However, resist the temptation to keep walking, as this may make your situation worse.

LOOKING FOR FEATURES

Stop and think through the route you have been taking. Identify on your map the last point at which you were sure of your location. Try to remember landmarks since your last known position and look for identifiable features. The view will be better from a ridge or a summit, so climb a little to reconnoiter, but go no further than you have to.

FINDING YOUR BEARINGS

Taking notice of obvious landmarks can help you locate your position if you become disorientated. In foggy weather, pay close attention to where you are.

USING YOUR MAP

When you have thought through your route and examined the terrain, take a close look at your map. Often, after a short rest and a little bit of thought, your location will become clear to you. If not, you will need to do some detective work. Apply the following steps, calmly and methodically, to help you pinpoint your position.

❶ Find your last-known position on the map as accurately as possible, and circle it.

❷ Estimate the length of time you have walked since your last-known position. Multiply your estimated travel time by your average speed to determine your maximum distance from your last-known position. Draw a circle with a radius of that distance. You are somewhere within this circle.

❸ Estimate a general direction of travel (if you have been walking toward the sun all evening, you can reasonably guess that you have traveled west). Draw a pie-shape area from your last known position out to the location circle in the general direction of travel.

❹ Look for features (such as a lake or a meadow) within the pie-shape section on your map that match features you remember passing earlier on your route.

❺ Find your likely position by looking for features on the map that match the current terrain. If you can identify surrounding landmarks on the map, you can triangulate your position (see p.79).

❻ If you have an altimeter, remember that your elevation is also a clue to where you are. Your location will be along one of the contour lines that matches the elevation shown by the altimeter.

❼ Look on your map for a large, identifiable feature that you can easily walk to from your likely position. An example might be that by walking northwest for a short distance you will reach a road. Then look for a prominent landmark along the road (such as a junction) that will pinpoint your location exactly.

❽ When you reach the landmark, work out how to return to your original route and continue as planned.

FINDING YOUR POSITION ON THE MAP

Establish your likely position by estimating the distance and direction of travel. Confirm your location by walking to a known point on the map.

Pinpoint a prominent feature outside the location area that you can walk to

Location circle—you are lost somewhere within this circle

Road

Feature (Road junction)

Road

Path

Location circle
❷

Look for features on the map that match your current terrain

Lake

Use features that you passed to check your current position

Woodland

❺

❹

❸ ❶

Path

Pie-shape section narrows down the area you believe you are in

Estimated direction of travel based on position of sun and time of day

Begin by marking your last known position on the map

Using the terrain to find your way

It is much easier to pinpoint your position on a warm, sunny day in high mountains where the topography is obvious and dramatic, than when you are lost in thick fog on a wet day on featureless moorland. If you cannot locate your position by comparing your surroundings to a map, start walking until you get your bearings, letting the terrain be your guide.

CHECKING YOUR MAP

If you are unsure of your position, stop and take a good look at your map. Note an obvious feature (such as a river or road), which if you stumble upon it, will help you to work out where you are. If you do reach it, look for an intersecting landmark to pinpoint your exact position.

FOLLOWING A BEARING

Some types of terrain, such as grass-land, are easy cross-country walking. You should be able to take a bearing (*see* p.79) and follow it directly to your destination. However, tangled jungle undergrowth can be difficult to cross without a path. In these conditions, you may be forced to take a circuitous route.

USING ROADS

Unless an area is reserved for walking exclusively, roads are likely to cross it at frequent intervals. Roads usually lead to civilization, and there is always the chance that a driver will come by and offer help. Be aware, however, that a road might lead you considerably out of your way, or to a dead end. In mountains, following roads downhill will usually lead you out of the wilderness. If you note the features you pass, you may have enough information to identify your location on your map.

FOLLOWING WATER

An oft-repeated theory tells hikers to follow streams downhill when lost, the theory being that streams will eventually converge with other streams, become rivers, and lead to habitation. In practice, however, following a stream may not be the best choice. Streams often take precipitous plunges; they can be choked with vegetation or boulders; and, while they certainly lead downhill, they may not follow the quickest route. So before choosing a stream as your route, look at your map to see in which direction the streams flow, and if their routes are steep. In hot areas, following a dry stream bed may lead to habitation.

ACQUIRE SOME PERSPECTIVE

Climb a ridge from which you can get a good view of the surrounding terrain and identify prominent landmarks from which to triangulate. If you can identify two features, you can use your map and compass to figure out precisely where you are in relation to them (*see* p.79).

USE THE LANDSCAPE

These hikers have a great deal of information to help them identify their position on a map: the lake, the bare rock, the steep hill, and the forested areas.

FOLLOW ROADS TO INHABITED AREAS
Take roads leading downhill out of mountains. Even in remote areas, you will often find farms or homes where you can ask for help and identify your location.

FINDING YOUR ROUTE AGAIN
If you lose your path in dense terrain, try to retrace your steps until you reach a familiar place, such as the turn-off you missed or the trail you were supposed to take. If you can see your destination, do not be tempted to go straight toward it—unless you are in a flat area. In wilderness areas, a straight line is rarely the best or shortest route and may take

you over mountaintops, into ravines, or across raging rivers. Check your route on a map carefully before setting off.

CONTOURING AND DETOURING
Contouring is the practice of following a contour line around any hills or ridges between you and your destination, rather than climbing and descending them. Detouring avoids obstacles (such as hills, swamps, or thick vegetation) by going round them. Watch your compass to see how far off-course you are going as you detour around the obstacle—for example, if you walk a mile west to go around a hill, compensate by walking a mile east once you get past it.

CONSIDERING YOUR WATER SUPPLY
In arid lands, finding water is even more important than finding your way. Following a dry streambed downhill will lead you to both water and habitation. Travel cross-country to signs of human habitation, such as wells, stock tanks, electrical lines and pylons, and shacks, which will be located near a road.

AIMING OFF-COURSE

Following a compass bearing is never totally accurate, especially when traveling cross-country over rough terrain or through dense vegetation. Instead of arriving at the crossroads you expected, for example, you

might arrive at just a stretch of road, with no way of knowing which side of the junction you are. To avoid this situation, deliberately aim for a large feature on your map that is to one side or the other of your less-visible target.

1 Determine a bearing from your location to the spring. Then search your map for a bigger feature nearby—in this case, a large copse.

2 Adjust your bearing by a few degrees so that you are actually aiming for the more visible copse to the right of the spring.

3 When you arrive at the copse, you know that you need to turn left, and continue walking, to reach the spring.

Animal encounters

Seeing wildlife is often the highlight of a hiking trip. Bears and cougars can be dangerous, but animals such as deer, moose, and buffalo are also responsible for human injuries. Most animal encounters, however, are benign and you are likely to see only startled animals dashing for cover.

Meeting wild animals on the trail

In North America hikers may see bears, mountain lions, wolves, coyotes, buffalo, moose, and deer, along with a wide range of other large and medium-sized mammals. Knowing what to do when you are close to wild animals is important, not only for you but also for the animals.

WILD ANIMALS IN NORTH AMERICA

Contrary to popular belief, wolves—an endangered, reclusive species—are not a threat to hikers. Mountain lions, however, are increasingly seen near inhabited areas, and attacks on humans sometimes occur. The mountain lion (also called the puma, panther, or cougar) is shy and solitary. If you encounter one, give it time and space to retreat. Usually, it will do so. Otherwise cluster together with your companions and try to present a big, noisy group. If you are alone, make sure the lion can see your pack, which helps you to look bigger. If the lion approaches, wave trekking poles and shout. Never run or bend down, as this makes you a smaller target.

Deer, moose, bison (American buffalo), and elk are all large, wild animals that can potentially harm you. If they are cornered, or protecting their young, their hooves, antlers, and horns can be used as lethal weapons. Retreat if you see an animal becoming agitated, and give it plenty of room to leave the area.

Most bears will quickly retreat from humans, but if you surprise a mother bear with cubs, she may send them up a tree and then watch you cautiously from a safe distance. Do not step between the mother and the tree, or approach the cubs. A large detour, however far off the track, is preferable to an attack by a bear.

Black bears are not usually predatory (to humans), but they can be dangerous if they are surprised or cornered, or if they have young. If a black bear shows signs of predatory behavior, your best defense is to become as aggressive as possible. Stay with your hiking partner (to present a

NORTH AMERICAN BLACK BEAR

The common black bear ranges over much of the North American continent. Grizzlies are more rare, and also more dangerous. Polar bears, which mainly inhabit the arctic tundra, are rarely seen by hikers.

1 Keep food away from bears by hanging it from a tree branch. Tie one end of a 40-ft (12-m) length of rope around a large stone. Throw the stone over a tree branch 10–12 ft (3–4 m) high so the rope is hanging over the branch.

2 Untie the stone and attach your food bag to the rope. Hoist it into the air and tie a weight (such as a rock) to the other end of the rope. Use a trekking pole or long stick to push the weight up so that it is hanging even with the bag.

bigger threat to the bear), yell, and wave your hiking sticks. As a last resort, throw rocks to scare the bear away.

PROTECTING FOOD

Never keep food in your tent. Store it in a waterproof stuff sack and hang it in a tree, beyond the reach of bears, and at least 100 ft (30 m) from your sleeping area. In some regions, bears are skilled at finding food in trees, in which case you should store food in a bear box (a metal locker at a campsite), a bear-proof canister, or a bear-proof stuff sack (*see* p.45). Some parks provide bear poles for hanging food. A carabiner is useful for attaching food to the cables or ropes on bear poles. When camping in the wild, cook your meal before stopping for the night, then hike a few more miles to set up camp. This prevents any food smells from attracting animals to your sleeping area.

ANIMAL VISITORS

▣ Camp away from obvious animal paths, water sources, and animal signs (droppings, claw marks on trees, tracks, etc.).
▣ Avoid popular campsites, where animals are used to finding food.
▣ Do not feed wild animals at a campsite. They become dependent on human food and may stop feeding themselves or neglect their migratory instinct. When people leave the area out of season, the animals could starve.
▣ Report aggressive animal encounters to local authorities.

GRIZZLY BEAR PRECAUTIONS

Grizzly bears are potentially more dangerous to hikers than other bears, so take these precautions if hiking in areas where they live.

AVOIDING GRIZZLIES

■ Stay in a group—bears do not usually attack groups of more than four people.
■ Avoid areas where you find signs of bears—fresh claw marks on trees, the smell of carrion, smashed vegetation, decimated berry bushes, droppings, and disturbed earth.
■ Be especially alert near water, which masks sounds and smells. You may surprise a grizzly that has not seen, heard, or smelled you.
■ Make a noise so that the grizzly can hear you and leave the area before you have to confront it.
■ Carry pepper spray that is specially formulated to deter an attacking bear.

ENCOUNTERING A GRIZZLY

■ Look for trees that you can climb (adult grizzlies cannot climb trees).
■ Talk quietly, do not make direct eye contact, and give it plenty of time to leave.
■ Discharge your pepper spray, but only if the bear comes within 15 ft (5 m).
■ If you are attacked, do not run. Play dead instead. Bring your legs up to your chest (to protect your vital organs), tuck in your head, and protect the back of your neck with your hands. Most grizzly attacks are defensive, and playing dead shows the bear that you are not a threat.

FIRST AID

Common ailments

While beginner hikers often worry about major accidents, encounters
with dangerous animals, or dramatic storms, the fact is that most hikers
are far more likely to be affected by common ailments. Sometimes these
can escalate into major problems if not appropriately treated.

Treating basic conditions

Minor injuries can result when a hiker
over-exerts (i.e. muscle cramps) or
spends too long in hot conditions (i.e.
sunburn). Blisters, cuts, and scrapes

are also common, but easily treated.
If hiking alone, you should aim to be
self-sufficient by carrying a first-aid kit
for the treatment of basic injuries.

QUICK TIPS

AIMS

- Soothe pain by using
a dressing
- Prevent infection

HOW TO PREVENT

- Apply an adhesive
bandage or moleskin pad
over the area of discomfort
- Wear smooth, high-
wicking socks next to skin
- Ensure that boots fit
well and are broken in
- Remove boots and air
the feet during breaks

BLISTERS

Blisters are a primary cause of discomfort when hiking,
and occur when the skin is rubbed repeatedly against a
surface. A blister starts as a small, almost imperceptible
irritation and may first appear as a red spot.

1 Clean the area with sterile
water and dry gently.
2 If possible, pop the blister
with a sterile needle. While not
recommended normally, this is
advisable for hikers, because
the continued friction from
walking will pop the blister
sooner or later.
3 When you pop the blister, be
sure to clean, dry, and protect
the area properly to lessen the
risk of infection.

*Secure the
dressing with
tape to hold
it in place*

4 Adhesive bandages, padded
moleskin, or gel-like dressings
can all be used to protect skin.

QUICK TIPS

SYMPTOMS

- Tenderness, swelling,
and pain
- Blue-black color of skin

WARNING

Severe bruising may
indicate deeper damage,
such as a fracture (see
p.143) or an internal
injury, and require
further medical
attention.

BRUISING

Bruising results when an injury breaks the blood vessels
under the skin. When hiking, this can be caused by
falling against a rock or other obstruction.

*Reduce swelling
and pain with a
cold compress*

1 To reduce the swelling, if you
have access to cold running
water, ice, or snow, soak a cloth
and apply it to the injured
area. Hold it in place for
at least five minutes.
Re-apply frequently.
2 If possible,
elevate the
bruised
area to reduce the
blood flow to it.

CUTS AND GRAZES

Cuts and grazes can occur on a hike as a result of falls, bashing through vegetation, or scraping against rocks. Any break in the skin needs to be cleaned and covered to prevent germs from entering and causing infection.

Rinse wound to remove any dirt

1 Clean the wound by rinsing it in cold running water (if possible), and drying it throughly.
2 Apply an antibiotic ointment and bandage with an appropriate dressing. Adhesive bandages may be sufficient for small wounds. For larger scrapes, cover with a gauze dressing and hold in place with adhesive bandages.

CRAMPS

Cramps are common, especially in the early stages of a hike, and the pain can occur suddenly. It happens when a muscle is stressed repeatedly, particularly if the muscle is not receiving enough oxygen.

Pull the foot up toward the shin

To treat a cramp in the legs, stop, stretch, and massage the affected muscles. Drinking a sports drink with electrolytes may help, especially if you have been sweating heavily.

SUNBURN

Sunburn is a constant outdoor hazard, and can contribute to dehydration, sunstroke, and skin cancer. It can occur even on cloudy days, especially at high altitudes, where the thinner air provides less protection against UV rays. Reflection by snow increases the risk.

1 Move the sufferer out of the sun into a cool, shaded spot.
2 Give the victim water to sip. It is important to drink frequently, as sunburn is a dehydrating condition.
3 Soothe mild burns by applying sun cream or calamine lotion. Cold water sponged onto the skin with a soft cloth can relieve pain and discomfort.

IMPORTANT

Monitor exposure to the sun, and continue to re-apply sun protection lotion. If exposure is extended or there are signs of sunburn, wear clothes that cover the affected area.

Stings, bites, and plant poisons

While much of the natural world is not harmful to humans, some plants and animals have developed toxins that can cause severe reactions, especially in those who are allergic.

Stinging insects, venomous snakes, and poisonous plants are easily avoided most of the time—but, unfortunately, not always. Snake bites in particular require prompt attention.

QUICK TIPS

SYMPTOMS

- Sharp and piercing stinging sensation
- Swollen, red, or sore skin
- Pain at site
- Itchy, red rash

AIMS

- Remove sting
- Reduce swelling and pain with cold compress
- Watch for signs of an allergic reaction and anaphylactic shock

INSECT STINGS

Insect stings rarely cause more than temporary discomfort unless you are highly allergic. If you are, you should carry a bee sting kit to treat anaphylactic shock and instruct your hiking partners in its use.

1 The sting may be embedded in the skin. It can usually be scraped away (using the edge of a credit card, or a fingernail).
2 Place a cloth soaked in cold water on the injured skin.
3 The casualty should rest with the injured part elevated until swelling ceases.
4 If the casualty suffers a severe allergic reaction (anaphylactic shock), seek medical attention.

If you can see it, carefully scrape away the sting

IMPORTANT

A sting in the mouth or throat can cause swelling that blocks the airway. Treat with cold water, ice, or snow, and seek medical attention if swelling develops. Also note that severe local responses to stings or a reaction, such as a rash all over the body, indicate that you are becoming more sensitized and should carry a bee sting kit on future hikes.

QUICK TIPS

SYMPTOMS

- Swelling around the bite

AIMS

- Remove tick
- Watch for symptoms of infection and disease, such as Lyme Disease

LYME DISEASE

Carried by tiny ticks from deer, this disease can cause a "bull's-eye" rash, joint pain, fever, or flu-like symptoms. The disease is treated by antibiotics.

TICKS

Ticks are tiny creatures that attach themselves to humans and bite into the skin to suck blood. They carry disease and can cause infection, so should be removed as soon as possible. Lyme Disease is of most concern because it is increasingly common worldwide.

1 Watch for ticks by checking skin. Ticks swell to the size of a pea. Check warm, moist places such as under the arms.

2 Ticks are best removed with tweezers. You should try to pull a tick out whole by encouraging it to let go of your skin. Grasp the tick as close to the skin as possible, and pull it out gently.
3 Wash the area thoroughly with water or a disinfectant and keep it clean.
4 Put the tick in a small container, so that it can be checked for Lyme Disease.
5 If symptoms occur, contact a doctor for tests and antibiotics.

Grasp the head close to the skin and pull gently

SNAKE BITE

The danger of venomous snakes varies greatly worldwide. Suctioning with a snake-bite venom extractor may be of benefit if far from a hospital, but should not be attempted by an untrained person.

1 Try to identify the snake to facilitate later treatment.
2 Lay the casualty down. Reassure them and make sure they are comfortable. Not all bites from venomous snakes inject venom, and many inject only a small amount. The amount of venom is not necessarily in proportion to the size of the snake.
3 Immobilize the bite area. Put on a light compression bandage above the bite. This can slow the spread of venom.
4 Go for help, or assist the casualty in walking out, if necessary and possible.

Raise the level of the heart above the level of bite

Secure padding around injured limb to immobilize

COMMON VENOMOUS SNAKES

SNAKE	COUNTRY	TOXICITY
European adder	Europe, parts of Asia	moderately venomous (causes internal bleeding)
Viper	worldwide except Australia	moderately venomous (causes internal bleeding)
Cottonmouth (pit viper)	southeast US	very venomous (clots the blood)
Cobra	south Asia and Africa	very venomous (causes paralysis)
Diamondback (rattlesnake)	North America	extremely venomous (can kill within one hour)

STINGING PLANTS

There are many stinging plant varieties, but poison ivy and stinging nettles are two of the most common. Poison ivy is found worldwide and causes rashes that vary in severity—some may need medical treatment. Stinging nettles are found in many countries, but cause only a temporary stinging sensation. After contact with stinging nettles, apply a cold compress to the site to soothe the pain. Watch for an itchy red rash that indicates an allergic reaction.

1 After contact with poison ivy, immediately wash the area with cold water and apply an anti-poison ivy cream as soon as possible.
2 Get medical help as soon as you can.

POISON IVY

Medical emergencies

In the wilderness, a medical emergency can happen with devastating suddenness, and professional help may be far away. Steps can be taken to avoid minor ailments, but for a serious condition such as hypothermia, or a bad fall, practical first-aid skills are essential.

Dehydration and heat maladies

One of the biggest challenges you face when hiking is maintaining your body's balance of water, electrolytes, and temperature, while undertaking strenuous activity and sweating

excessively. This can be difficult in hot or humid weather, or when exposed to extreme conditions such as very dry air or high altitude. Make sure you drink water at every rest stop.

DEHYDRATION

Dehydration is commonly associated with strenuous exercise, particularly in hot weather. It is exacerbated by high altitude, heat, sun exposure, and by both extreme humidity and extreme dryness. Dehydration is dangerous in itself, but it can also contribute to heat exhaustion, heatstroke, and even hypothermia.

1 Find shade if possible, or make shade using a tarp.
2 Make the casualty comfortable and encourage them to slowly drink small amounts of water. Dilute an electrolyte-replacement drink to half the original strength and administer it in small amounts. Or you can make a solution by adding a tablespoon of sugar and a teaspoon of salt to two pints of water.
3 To prevent a relapse, identify causes. Common causes include diarrhea

or vomiting (from adverse food reactions or altitude sickness), overexertion (especially at high altitude and in dry air), and sun exposure.
4 Encourage rest until the casualty is fully recovered.

Support the casualty while they sip slowly

ELECTROLYTES

Electrolytes are mineral salts in the body that move between body cells. One function of the kidneys is to keep these salts in balance. This balance is essential for the functioning of body processes such as heart and nerve function, muscle coordination, and bone

health. When you are on a hard hike you lose electrolytes as you sweat. To help replace this loss, some drinks have electrolytes (such as sodium and potassium) added to them to help the kidneys keep the electrolyte concentrations in your body fluids constant.

HEATSTROKE

Heatstroke can develop suddenly. The body's heat-regulating mechanisms break down completely and the body is unable to cool itself by sweating, so it becomes dangerously overheated. The skin will feel hot and may be either damp from perspiration (if the victim was exercising), or dry. A heatstroke victim should be cooled down and taken to a hospital quickly.

1 Move the casualty to as cool a place as possible and protect them from the sun.
2 Maintain an open airway if the casualty is unconscious.
3 Do anything possible to reduce the temperature quickly. Sponge the body with cool or cold water and try to fan the casualty, using clothing or equipment to help move air. An unconscious victim can be covered with clothing soaked in cold water. Immersion in cool

or cold water is recommended for conscious victims.
4 Massage extremities to encourage blood circulation. Once temperature has dropped, replace the wet clothes with dry ones.
5 Monitor the level of response, pulse, and breathing.

Fan the casualty to lower temperature

QUICK TIPS

SYMPTOMS

■ Confusion and impaired mental function
■ Headache or dizziness
■ High body temperature—above 104°F (40°C)
■ Flushed, very hot skin
■ Fast, strong pulse

AIMS

■ Stabilize victim—cool them as quickly as possible
■ Seek medical attention

WARNING

Under no circumstances should a victim of heatstroke resume activity until they have been medically evaluated. Severe organ damage is possible, and relapse is common, even after several hours.

HEAT EXHAUSTION

Heat exhaustion occurs in heat and humidity, especially when hikers are not used to such conditions. Blood vessels in the skin dilate and the blood supply to the brain lessens, causing dizziness and possibly fainting. Heat exhaustion can sometimes develop into heatstroke.

1 Help the casualty to sit or lie down, preferably in a cool or shaded place. Make them comfortable and raise the legs to improve blood flow to the brain.
2 Give plenty of water or non-carbonated drinks to replace lost fluids. Include diluted electrolyte replacement drinks, if available.
3 Reduce the body temperature with a cool compress (such as a handkerchief soaked in water), and by fanning.

4 Make sure the casualty rests until body temperature and urine output are normal.
5 Monitor the casualty's condition because heat exhaustion can turn into potentially lethal heatstroke. If it does not improve, seek medical attention. Immediate medical attention should always be sought for those who have chronic conditions such as heart or kidney disease, which could be exacerbated by heat exhaustion.

QUICK TIPS

SYMPTOMS

■ Cramplike pains
■ Damp, pale skin
■ Headache and confusion
■ Decreased urine output
■ Nausea and fainting
■ Raised body temperature
■ Fast, weak pulse

AIMS

■ Cool the casualty
■ Make them comfortable
■ Encourage rest
■ Replace lost body fluids
■ Obtain medical help, if necessary

Altitude sickness, frostbite, and hypothermia

Although ailments caused by cold are more common in winter, they are a possibility at any time of year in high mountains, where both the elevation and cold climate can stress the human body. Treatment is necessary to restore normal body temperature and breathing as rapidly as possible.

ALTITUDE SICKNESS

Everyone responds to altitude differently, but one thing is consistent—the higher you go, the more likely you are to be affected by the lack of oxygen in the thinner air. Many hikers feel symptoms of altitude sickness above 10,000 ft (3,000 m). Once you reach this height, avoid gaining more than 1,000 ft (300 m) a day. Most hikers feel some effects above 12,000 ft (3,600 m). Acute Mountain Sickness (AMS), can result in cerebral or pulmonary oedema (waterlogged brain or lungs).

QUICK TIPS

SYMPTOMS

■ Mild—breathlessness, headaches, nausea, dizziness, insomnia
■ Serious—confusion, lack of coordination, vomiting, dry cough

HOW TO PREVENT

■ Choose a pace that allows plenty of time for acclimatization
■ Drink extra fluids to avoid dehydration
■ Eat light, high-carbohydrate meals at frequent intervals and avoid alcohol

1 Treat mild symptoms by resting at the same altitude for a day or two.
2 If symptoms persist, go downhill to the last altitude where the casualty felt well.
3 Hikers with serious symptoms should descend immediately and seek medical treatment, which usually includes extra oxygen.

> **IMPORTANT**
>
> If mild symptoms persist for more than a day or two, or become worse, it is important to descend immediately—even 1,500 ft (500 m) can help.

FROSTBITE

Frostbite is usually a winter injury. The tissues of the extremities—such as fingers and toes—freeze because of low temperatures. Trekkers in high mountains may be at risk if under-equipped during a summer snowstorm.

QUICK TIPS

SYMPTOMS

■ Prickling pain or redness of the skin
■ Numbness
■ Skin feels hard and waxy to the touch
■ Skin can turn white, then blue or black

AIMS

■ Warm affected areas very slowly
■ Prevent further freezing
■ Seek medical treatment immediately

> **IMPORTANT**
>
> In severe cases, frostbite can cause permanent damage or loss of the affected tissue. If symptoms occur, it is important to seek medical attention.

1 If possible, take the casualty to a warm place and remove wet or constricting clothing.
2 Use body heat to warm the area. Frostbitten fingers can be warmed by putting them under the arms or against the stomach. Or, if toes or feet are frostbitten, a hiking partner's armpits or stomach can be used to warm them. Do not, however, thaw a frostbitten foot if the casualty needs to walk further.
3 Do not use anything hot such as heating pads, a stove, or hot water because the casualty may not be able to feel burning sensations.
4 Avoid rubbing or massaging the affected area as this can further damage the skin.

5 After warming, loosely bandage the area to protect it. Keep the area bandaged until feeling returns to the skin.

Tuck frostbitten hands in armpits to generate body heat

HYPOTHERMIA

Hypothermia is sometimes called the "killer of the unprepared." Cold is not just a winter problem—a hiker on a cool rainy day can be even more susceptible than a winter skier if he or she does not have the appropriate rain and wind protection. Rain and dampness exacerbate the danger, because wet, cold air takes warmth away from the skin much faster than dry, cold air. Hunger and fatigue can also contribute.

1 Remove the casualty from wind or rain by choosing a sheltered spot or erecting a shelter such as a tent. Make them comfortable, using clothing, backpacks, or sleeping mats to insulate them from the cold ground and to prevent further heat loss.
2 Warm the casualty slowly—remove wet or damp clothing (cut it away to avoid jostling the casualty). Replace with dry, insulated clothing or sleeping bags.
3 Administer warm drinks slowly to a conscious victim.

4 Ensure the casualty rests.
5 For casualties with severe hypothermia, seek medical help.

Give warm liquids, but not alcohol

Provide reassurance and comfort

A hat gives extra warmth

Protect from rain and wind with a survival bag

PREVENTING HYPOTHERMIA

It is very important to dress correctly for cool conditions. You should be able to add or remove layers according to your activity level and the outside temperature. Wearing clothing in multiple layers means that you can control your temperature and avoid heavy sweating. Carry warm hats, extra socks, scarves, raingear, gloves, and a survival blanket. Nibble high-energy foods, such as energy bars and nuts, and carry enough fluid. The warning sign of hypothermia is prolonged and uncontrolled shivering. You must act immediately to prevent severe hypothermia, which can be fatal.

Injury

It only takes a moment's lack of attention to slip on a wet rock or fall off a boulder that unexpectedly shifts underfoot. The result can be a nasty cut, or a more serious fall or jolt can lead to a broken bone or dislocation. Whatever the outcome, you will need to carry out some form of first aid.

SPRAINS AND STRAINS

Sprains and strains are much less likely to occur if you stretch regularly as part of your exercise regime. Flexible joints are more likely to be able to absorb the sudden twists, jolts, and falls that can happen to a hiker on tricky terrain. A strain is a torn muscle or tendon, and is caused when the muscle is overstretched. A sprain occurs when the ligament that supports the joint is stretched or torn. Ankles are especially prone to this happening, which is one reason that heavily laden hikers wear boots with strong ankle support. Sprains and strains can be extremely painful and indistinguishable from fractures without an x-ray. If in doubt, they should be treated as a fracture.

Sprained ligament at ankle

Painful swelling and bruising

SPRAINED ANKLE

IMPORTANT

Treat sprains and strains initially with the RICE (rest, ice, compression, and elevation) procedure, explained below. If you are unsure about the severity of the injury, treat it as a fracture instead, and immobilize the injury. If one leg is injured, bandage this leg to the sound one, using triangular bandages above and below the sprain or fracture site.

1 Rest—For complete healing, the injured part needs to rest. In an isolated area, the casualty may have to leave on foot. Assist by carrying as much of their backpacking load as possible. When at rest, steady and support the injured part.

2 Ice—Cool the area to reduce pain and swelling by applying ice or snow if available. If it is not, use a cloth soaked in cold water, lightly applied around the injured area.

3 Compress—Apply gentle pressure to the injured joint. Surround the area with a layer of thick, soft padding, then secure with an elastic bandage. Wrap in a figure-eight pattern (around the forefoot, then the ankle, then looping back) to support the joint. Check that there is adequate circulation in the toes.

4 Elevate—Raise the injury, if possible above the heart. This helps reduce swelling and bruising by helping the body to absorb blood and body fluids.

Reduce swelling at the ankle with ice or a cold cloth

2 Ice

Compress with a bandage

3 Compress

DISLOCATION

Dislocation occurs when a bone is forced out of its normal position by a wrenching jolt. It is an extremely painful injury that may also affect the surrounding nerves. Commonly affected areas of the body are shoulders, fingers (especially the thumb), and jaw.

Dislocation can have serious consequences. Dislocations of the hip or shoulder may damage the large nerves to the arm or leg, resulting in paralysis. Any dislocation may also be accompanied by a fracture of the adjacent bone.

A dislocated thumb is a common injury when hiking

DISLOCATED JOINT

1 Advise the casualty to stay still, and support the joint in as comfortable a position as possible.
2 Immobilize the injured joint using padding, bandages, and slings. Do not move the casualty until the injured part is secured and supported, unless the casualty is in danger.
3 If it is a shoulder dislocation, secure the arm against the chest using a bandage.
4 Treat the casualty for shock, if necessary (*see* p.145), and seek medical help.

QUICK TIPS

SYMPTOMS

■ Contorted limbs
■ Possible swelling around the joint
■ Pain aggravated by motion
■ Bruising

AIMS

■ Immobilize the joint to reduce pain
■ Arrange transportation with comfortable support to the hospital

WARNING

Do not attempt to reposition a dislocated bone into its socket. This may cause further injury, especially if there is also a fracture or nerve damage. Seek medical help.

BROKEN BONES

Fractures and breaks are traumatic injuries to the bones. In some cases, pieces of bone may break through skin; in others, an x-ray may be required to identify the injury as a fracture. If an injury is severe enough to cause fracturelike symptoms, it should be assumed to be a fracture for first-aid purposes.

1 First, immobilize the bone by splinting the joint. This helps to decrease pain, reduce shock and bleeding, and prevent further damage. Almost anything can be used as a splint, from part of a foam pad or a trekking pole, to a stick or a rolled-up magazine.
2 The limb may need to be straightened before being splinted—this should be done as soon as possible after the accident. Protect protruding bones such as an elbow or knee with cloth or bandages.

3 Support the injured part with a sling or by bandaging it to an unaffected part of the body. Check regularly for feeling in the extremities, to be sure that the splint or bandage is not too tight.

Use a bandage or sling to immobilize the injured part and keep the splint in place

QUICK TIPS

SYMPTOMS

■ Pain
■ Inability to move, or difficulty in moving, the limb
■ Swelling and discoloration
■ Shortening, bending, or twisting of a limb
■ Visible deformity of bones or bones breaking through skin
■ Signs of shock (*see* p.145)

AIMS

■ Immobilize joint to prevent movement in the area of injury
■ Protect protruding bones
■ Reduce pain
■ Control bleeding from wounds by elevation
■ Get transportation to the hospital, with comfortable support during travel

BLEEDING

Bleeding often looks drastic and dramatic. Except in the case of highly unusual and severe injuries, it can usually be slowed or stopped by a combination of elevation and direct pressure. Do not use a tourniquet as this can be dangerous. In remote areas, an additional challenge is keeping the injured area and any dressings as clean as possible. Victims of severe bleeding injuries should also be treated for shock.

1 If the skin is torn, place your hands on either side and push the edges together, while placing direct pressure on the wound. Most wounds are of capillaries and veins, and will clot after several minutes of direct pressure. Arterial bleeding takes longer because the arteries are under more pressure. However, arterial injuries are less common.
2 If the bone is not broken and the patient can be moved, lie them down comfortably and raise the affected limb. Direct pressure on the wound should be maintained. Use a gauze pad to absorb the blood. Even if the wound does not completely stop bleeding, it can still be bandaged and wrapped.

Push the edges of the wound together to stop the bleeding

Elevate the legs above the level of the heart

Raise the limb, maintaining direct pressure on the injury

3 Apply a sterile dressing. Place a gauze pad over the wound, and hold it in place by wrapping bandages around the limb. If blood seeps through the dressing, add another pad.
4 Continue to apply pressure, if necessary, and keep the wounded area elevated. Support the injured limb in a raised position with a sling or bandage.

5 The dressing should not be so tight that it restricts circulation. Check frequently that there is adequate circulation below the bandage. Check for a pulse, and look at fingernail and skin color (bluish skin indicates lack of circulation). Ask about tingling sensations, pain, or numbness.
6 If the dressing is too tight, take off the bandage, then reapply.

7 Remove the bandage after the bleeding has stopped. Dress the wound in clean bandages, which should be changed daily.
8 Movement of the wounded area should be restricted, even after bleeding has stopped, because excessive movement and jostling can cause the wound to open. If the casualty must leave, splint the wounded area.

Shock

Shock occurs when the circulatory system fails, and as a result, vital organs such as the heart and the brain are deprived of oxygen. Shock can be life-threatening. It requires emergency treatment to prevent organ damage, and casualties must be referred to a medical professional for follow-up care.

TREATING SHOCK

The underlying cause of the shock should be treated first. Shock is commonly caused by severe blood loss. It can also be a result of fluid loss caused by severe burns, fractures, heatstroke, or hypothermia. Symptoms do not always appear immediately, so you should treat for shock regardless of symptoms in cases of major blood loss, unconsciousness, and severe heat- and cold-related disorders.

1 Lie the casualty down. The head should be at the same level as the body or lower, and the feet raised 10–12 in (25–30 cm). If possible, lie the casualty on a camping mat to prevent loss of heat, and provide shelter from wind and cold, either with natural windbreaks or by erecting a tarp or tent.
2 Maintain the body temperature of the casualty. Sleeping bags and extra clothing may not be enough—an external source of heat such as a fire or another person's body heat may be required. Loosen any restrictive clothing around the body.
3 Keep the casualty calm. Panic, fear, and pain can increase the severity of shock. Do not move the casualty until the the cause of shock has been treated and it has been controlled. Monitor the casualty's breathing, pulse rate, and level of consciousness. If possible, also monitor their heart rate, temperature, urine output, and blood pressure.

QUICK TIPS

SYMPTOMS

- Fast, weak pulse
- Pallor
- Cool skin
- Chills
- Lack of urination
- Mental confusion

AIMS

- Stabilize condition
- Keep casualty warm and comfortable
- Monitor condition
- Keep notes
- Seek medical attention

IMPORTANT

It is vital to seek urgent medical treatment. Shock victims will need to be monitored until help arrives, as their condition can deteriorate quickly.

Monitor the casualty's pulse rate

Raise legs to improve blood supply to vital organs

Keep the casualty warm

Keep legs elevated above the level of the heart

Dealing with unconsciousness

Unconsciousness can result from a number of disorders, including illness such as heart attack, diabetes, and seizures, trauma, hypothermia, altitude sickness, and the later stage of heatstroke. If you are in a very remote area, medical help may be far away and difficult to contact. The victim's survival can depend on your ability to perform life-saving techniques, summon emergency help, and arrange an evacuation.

QUICK TIPS

SYMPTOMS

■ The victim does not respond to stimuli
■ Breathing and pulse may have ceased

AIMS

■ Get help
■ Assess the victim's response
■ Establish and maintain an open, clear airway
■ Check for breathing and give rescue breaths (see p.147) if necessary
■ Check for signs of circulation and give chest compressions (see p.148) if necessary
■ Stabilize the victim: deal with severe injuries or medical conditions, then place in the recovery position (see p.149). Monitor and keep a record, if possible, of the victim's pulse, breathing, and level of response
■ Protect the victim from extremes of weather

REVIVING AN UNCONSCIOUS PERSON

A person who is unconscious is in danger of their airway being blocked, especially if the tongue falls into the back of the throat. If the airway is blocked, the person is unable to breathe, so opening it up quickly is a vitally important early action.

1 Look for any danger to yourself or the victim, such as loose rocks, as you approach the scene and deal with it if necessary.
2 Check for a response by speaking loudly and clearly to the victim and gently shaking the shoulders. Use the person's name if you know it.
3 Shout for help—there may be someone else hiking in the area.
4 Open the airway by placing one hand on the forehead and tilting the head back, removing any obvious obstruction from the mouth and lifting the chin. Check for breathing by looking along the victim's chest for movement, listening for breath sounds, and feeling for breath on your cheek. Do this for ten seconds.
5 If the victim is not breathing, send for emergency help if possible, and start rescue breathing (see p.147).
6 If the victim is breathing, stablize them by dealing with any severe injuries or known medical conditions. Place them in the recovery position (see p.149).
7 Monitor pulse, breathing, and level of response until help arrives. Protect the victim from weather by erecting a shelter. Do not leave the victim unless there is no other way of getting help.

Speak to the victim and shake gently to assess whether they are conscious or unconscious

Check for signs of circulation—breathing, coughing, or movement

RESCUE BREATHING

If the victim is not breathing, it is very important to send for emergency help if possible and then start rescue breathing. The organs of the body—especially the brain—start to suffer damage from lack of oxygen very quickly. Rescue breathing is an effective way of giving some oxygen to a victim who is not breathing. Your exhaled breath contains about 16 percent oxygen— 5 percent less than air but still a very useful amount for someone who is not breathing. Rescue breaths force air into the lungs of the victim, from where it is carried around the body to organs, including the brain.

1 Open the airway. Place one hand on the victim's forehead and gently tilt the head back. Remove any obstructions, such as vomit or dentures, from the mouth and lift the chin.
2 Keeping the airway open, pinch the nose closed with the fingers of the hand on the forehead. This prevents air from escaping through the nostrils.
3 Take a deep breath and seal your mouth over the victim's mouth.
4 To start, give two rescue breaths. If the chest does not rise, adjust the airway and try again. Make five attempts to give two effective breaths (the chest should rise and fall fully). This takes around six seconds.
5 After each breath, take your mouth off the victim's mouth to allow air to escape.
6 After giving two initial breaths, check for signs of circulation— breathing, coughing, and movement. If signs are apparent, go to step 7. If no signs are apparent, go to step 10.
7 Continue giving long, slow rescue breaths at a rate of ten breaths per minute.
8 Check circulation after every minute. If circulation ceases at any point, administer cardio-pulmonary resuscitation, or CPR (*see* p.148). CPR combines rescue breathing with chest compressions.
9 If the victim begins to breathe again, stabilize them and—if the victim can be moved—place in the recovery position (*see* p.149).
10 If there are no signs of circulation, begin CPR immediately (*see* p.148).

Tilt victim's head back and support the jaw with the index and middle fingers

Seal lips over victim's mouth while pinching their nose

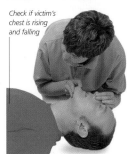

Check if victim's chest is rising and falling

CHILD TECHNIQUE

The rescue breathing procedure is slightly different for a child:
■ Open the airway by doing head tilt and chin lift as for an adult.
■ Pinch the nose, take a deep breath, and seal your mouth over the victim's.
■ Give two initial rescue breaths at a rate of one every three seconds. Make sure the chest rises and falls fully.
■ After the two initial breaths, look for signs of circulation—breathing, coughing, and movement.
■ If those signs are present, continue rescue breaths at a rate of 20 per minute. After every minute, recheck for circulation.
■ If those signs are not present or disappear, start CPR (*see* p.148).

WARNING

When giving rescue breaths, it is good practice to be as hygienic as possible so that you help to prevent the spread of infectious diseases. This can be done by using disposable gloves and a plastic face shield (a barrier with a reinforced mouthpiece that fits over the mouth of the victim). These items are portable, lightweight, and small enough to be included in a hiking first aid kit.

CPR

Cardiopulmonary resuscitation (CPR) is a combination of chest compressions and rescue breathing (*see* p.147). The procedure is applied to a victim who is not breathing and has no circulation. CPR stimulates blood flow to the brain and ventilates the lungs. This procedure is taught worldwide in courses offered by many organizations, including the Red Cross. The specific procedures vary depending on the age of the victim (*see* Child Technique, *below*) and the number of people involved in the rescue. If two rescuers are present, one can administer the rescue breathing while the other does the chest compressions. If only one rescuer is present, he or she must alternate between rescue breathing and chest compressions.

Place middle and index fingers on breastbone

1 Open the airway and give two rescue breaths (*see* p.147). Then find the point on the chest where the lowermost rib meets the breastbone. Place the middle finger and index finger of one hand there.

Position heel of other hand above fingers

2 Put the heel of the second hand next to the two fingers that are on the breastbone. This is where you will apply pressure during the compressions.

Lock fingers firmly together

3 Place the first hand on top of the second hand and interlock the fingers.

Keep your arms straight and press down with heel of your hand

HANDS ON CHEST

4 Give 30 chest compressions by pushing down 1¹/₂–2 inches (4–5 cm) at a rate of 100 per minute.

CHILD TECHNIQUE

The procedure is slightly different for a child.
■ Give one rescue breath, then administer five chest compressions with one hand only.
■ Continue the cycle of one breath to five compressions.

5 Give two rescue breaths followed by 30 compressions.
6 Continue the cycle of two rescue breaths and 30 compressions until the victim recovers, help arrives, or it becomes impossible to continue. If you are in a very remote area, professional medical assistance may not be available. Therefore, it is very important that you carry on with the cycle of chest compressions and rescue breaths until you are exhausted, so that you give the victim the best chance of survival.

Pinch nose and seal lips over mouth

RECOVERY POSITION

If breathing and heartbeat are present, the unconscious person will need to be stabilized (*see* p.146), until evacuation can be arranged. If you are hiking in a group, one or two members of the party can go for help, while others stay with the victim. Do not hesitate to seek help from other hikers in the area.

Once the victim has been stabilized, he or she should be put in the recovery position (*see below*), which promotes clear breathing, good blood circulation, and keeps the victim resting comfortably until help arrives. The position, however, should be used only with victims who can be moved safely.

1 Kneel beside the victim and straighten the victim's legs. Remove any bulky items from the victim's pockets.
2 Place the victim's arm that is closest to you at a right angle to the body, with the hand facing upward (as if the victim was waving at someone).
3 Put the arm farthest from you across their chest and hold the hand palm outward against the victim's cheek closest to you.
4 Grasping the thigh of the leg that is farthest from you, pull the

leg up until the foot is flat on the floor. Pull the leg toward you and roll the victim onto their side.
5 At the end of the maneuver, the victim should be lying on one side, with the bottom leg extended and the top leg bent at the hip and the knee in a comfortable position. Be sure that the victim is stable and cannot roll onto their back.
6 Check that the victim is breathing evenly, and that the airway is not obstructed.

SEEKING HELP

■ Use a cell phone to call emergency services, if possible. Climb to a high ridge, or try in several locations, as reception in hiking areas may be bad.
■ If you have to walk out to find help, check your map to find the quickest route.
■ Take notes with you that list the victim's vital signs (breathing and pulse), any evident injuries, and what first aid procedures you have performed.
■ Mark your location precisely on a map and take it with you so rescuers do not have to waste time searching for the victim.

Hand under cheek helps to keep head tilted and airway open

Bottom leg is extended

Top arm is bent so that cheek rests on back of hand

Bottom arm is bent at elbow and palm faces up

Top leg is bent at hip and knee

WARNING

There are certain situations when placing a victim in the recovery position is not recommended.
■ If head, neck, or spinal trauma is suspected, the victim's body should not be moved, but the jaw can be pulled forward to position the tongue so it is less likely to obstruct the airway.
■ If a victim is in the late stages of hypothermia, movement could cause heart fibrillation (a life-threatening rhythm disturbance in the heart), but you should make sure the airway is not blocked.

In both cases, you must pay close and continual attention to the victim's breathing, because the tongue of an unconscious person can fall back into the airway and block the passage of air.
■ If, however, you have no choice but to leave the victim unattended while you go for help, you should use the recovery position to reduce the chance of airway obstruction. Move the victim as gently as possible. In the case of head, neck, and spinal injuries, try to keep the victim's spine completely straight and supported during the maneuver.

Resources

Whether you are looking for a hiking club in your area, searching for a destination for your first overnight hike, or preparing for a multiweek expedition, this section provides you with phone numbers, addresses, and web links to help you find the information you will need.

ONLINE RESOURCES

American Hiking Society
1422 Fenwick Lane
Silver Spring, MD 20910
Tel: 301-565-6704
Web: www.americanhiking.org
National organization dedicated to serving hikers and protecting trails.

Gorp.com
www.gorp.com
Comprehensive guide to hiking and backpacking, including hikes, gear guides, expert tips, and more.

Local Hikes
www.localhikes.com
Information on hikes close to major metropolitan areas across the United States.

Webwalking
www.webwalking.com/hiking.asp
This online guide offers information on hikes, gear, tours, long-distance treks, and more.

US HIKING ORGANIZATIONS

Organizations are ordered alphabetically, by state.

ALABAMA
Alabama Hiking Trail Society
P.O. Box 231164, Montgomery
AL 36123
Tel: 334-239-3210
Email: ahts@hikealabama.org
Web: www.alabamatrail.com
Dedicated to the development and maintenance of a connected system of trails through the state of Alabama.

ALASKA
Trail Mix, Inc.
P.O. Box 35493. Juneau, AK 99803
Tel: 907-790-6406
Email: info@juneautrails.org
Web: www.juneautrails.org
An organization that organizes trail improvements and activities.

ARIZONA
Arizona Trail Association
P.O. Box 36736, Phoenix
AZ 85067-6736
Tel: 602-252-4794
Email: ata@aztrail.org
Web: www.aztrail.org
Coordinates the planning and development of the Arizona Trail.

ARKANSAS
Ozark Highlands Trail Association
HC 33, Box 50-A, Pettigrew, AR 72752
Tel: 870-861-5536
Email: Timernst@timernst.com
Web: www.hikearkansas.com
Maintains the Ozark Highlands Trail.

CALIFORNIA
High Sierra Hikers Association
P.O. Box 8920, South Lake Tahoe
CA 96158
Email: HSHAhike@aol.com
Web: www.highsierrahikers.org
Dedicated to preserving and protecting the trails and wilderness of the High Sierra mountains.

Santa Monica Mountains Trails Council
Box 345, Agoura Hills, CA 91376
Tel: 818-222-4531
Email: mail@smmtc.org
Web: www.smmtc.org
Maintains the public trail system throughout the Santa Monica Mountains, near Los Angeles.

COLORADO
Colorado Trail Foundation
710 10th Street, #210
Golden, CO 80401-5843
Tel: 303-384-3729
Email: ctf@coloradotrail.org
Web: www.coloradotrail.org
Maintains the Colorado Trail, a 486-mile route from Denver to Durango.

CONNECTICUT
Meshomasic Hiking Club
460 Chamberlain Road, Middletown
CT 06457
Tel: 860-347-0349
Email: meshomasic@sbcglobal.net
Web: www.geocities.com/meshomasic
Aims to help its members enjoy hikes and trails throughout the state.

FLORIDA
Florida Trail Association
5415 SW 13th Street
Gainesville, FL 32608
Tel: 877-HIKE-FLA
Email: fta@florida-trail.org
Web: www.florida-trail.org
Dedicated to maintaining and promoting hiking trails, with a special focus on the 1,400-mile Florida Trail.

GEORGIA
Georgia Appalachian Trail Club
P.O. Box 654, Atlanta, GA 30301
Tel: 404-634-6495
Email: president@georgia-atclub.org
Web: www.georgia-atclub.org
Maintains the Georgia section of the Appalachian Trail, as well as other trails in the state.

HAWAII
E Mau Na Ala Hele
P.O. Box 6384, Kamuela, HI 96743
Tel: 808-328-8911
Email: mcshort50@yahoo.com
Web: www.alakahakai.com
An advocacy group for ancient and historic trails in Hawaii.

ILLINOIS
River to River Trail Society
1142 Winkleman Road
Harrisburg, IL 62946
Tel: 618-252-6789
Email: trails444@hotmail.com
Web: www.rivertorivertrail.com
Maintains and promotes the River to River Trail across southern Illinois.

INDIANA
Indianapolis Hiking Club
871 W. Fairview Road, Greenwood
IA 46142
Tel: 317-388-0498
Email: malayman@earthlink.net
Web: www.indyhike.org
Organizes hikes in the Indianapolis area, with over 1,000 hikes annually.

KANSAS

Kansas Trails Council
PO Box 695, Topeka,
KS 66601-0695
Tel: 316-321-2267
Email: goodwinmw@cox.net
Web: www.terraworld.net/
  kansastrails
*Maintains and develops trails
throughout Kansas.*

KENTUCKY

Pine Mountain Trail Conference
P.O. Box 784
Whitesburg, KY 41858
Tel: 606-633-2362
Email: sbaker@uky.edu
Web: www.pinemountaintrail.com
*Currently developing the Pine
Mountain Trail along the Kentucky-
Virginia border.*

LOUISIANA

Louisiana Hiking Club
9605 Jefferson Hwy, River Ridge
LA 70123
Tel: 504-491-9932
Email: tomrogers@ureach.com
Web: www.hikelouisiana.org
*Dedicated to maintaining trails,
organizing hikes, and promoting the
natural resources of the state.*

MINNESOTA

Parks and Trails Council of Minnesota
275 Fourth Street East 642
St. Paul, MN 55101
Tel: 651-726-2457
Email: info@parksandtrails.org
Web: www.parksandtrails.org
*Seeks to acquire, protect, and
enhance trails and natural lands.*

MISSOURI

Ozark Trail Association
483 South Kirkwood Road, #40
Kirkwood, MO 63122
Tel: 573-786-2065
Email: ota.volunteer@gmail.com
Web: www.ozarktrail.com
*A volunteer group dedicated to the
development, maintenance, and
promotion of the Ozark Trail.*

NEVADA

Tahoe Rim Trail Association
948 Incline Way
Incline Village, NV 89451
Tel: 775-298-0012
Email: info@tahoerimtrail.org

Web: www.tahoerimtrail.org
*Dedicated to the expansion,
maintenance, and promotion
of the Tahoe Rim Trail System.*

NEW HAMPSHIRE

Randolph Mountain Club
P.O. Box 279, Gorham, NH 03581
Email:
  info@randolphmountainclub.org
Web: www.randolphmountainclub.org
*Promotes and develops trails in the
Northern White Mountains of New
Hampshire.*

NEW JERSEY

Outdoor Club Of South Jersey
35 Hoton Lane, Willingboro
NJ 08046
Tel: 609-877-7018
Email: info@ocsj.org
Web: www.ocsj.org
*A non-profit organization that
provides low-cost outdoor activities
in and around southern New Jersey.*

NEW MEXICO

**New Mexico Volunteers for
the Outdoors**
P.O. Box 36246, Albuquerque
NM 87176
Tel: 505-884-1991
Email: promotions@nmufo.org
Web: www.nmvfo.org
*Volunteer trail maintenance group in
the state of New Mexico.*

See also **New York–New Jersey Trail
Conference**

NEW YORK

Adirondack Mountain Club
814 Goggins Road, Lake George
NY 12845-4117
Tel: 518-668-4447
Email: adkinfo@adk.org
Web: www.adk.org
*Organization dedicated to the
protection and responsible use of the
New York State Forest Preserve, parks,
and other wild lands and waters.*

Finger Lakes Trail Conference
6111 Visitor Center Road
Mount Morris, NY 14510-9527
Tel: 585-658-9320
Email: FLTinfo@fingerlakestrail.org
Web: www.fingerlakestrail.org
*Builds and maintains a continuous
footpath across New York State.*

**Long Island Greenbelt
Trail Conference**
P.O. Box 5636
Hauppauge, NY 11788-0141
Tel: 631-360-0753
Email: ligreenbelt@verizon.net
Web: www.hike-ligreenbelt.com
*Dedicated to preserving open
spaces and maintaining hiking
trails throughout Long Island.*

**New York–New Jersey Trail
Conference**
156 Ramapo Valley Road
Mahwah, NJ 07430-1199
Tel: 201-512-9348
Email: office@nynjtc.org
Web: www.nynjtc.org
*Maintains and promotes trails in
New York and northern New Jersey.*

NORTH CAROLINA

Carolina Mountain Club
P.O. Box 68, Asheville, NC 28802
Tel: 828-236-0192
Email: cmcinfo@carolinamtnclub.org
Web: www.carolinamtnclub.org
*A club dedicated to exploring the
mountains of western North Carolina.*

OHIO

Buckeye Trail Association
P.O. Box 254, Worthington, OH 43085
Tel: 740-585-2603
Email: info@buckeyetrail.org
Web: www.buckeyetrail.org
*Maintains and develops the 1,300-
mile Buckeye Trail.*

OREGON

Jacksonville Woodlands Association
P.O. Box 1210, Jacksonville, OR 97530
Tel: 541-899-7402
Email: info@jvwoodlands.org
Web: www.jvwoodlands.org
*Preserves land and creates trail
systems near Jacksonville in
southern Oregon.*

PENNSYLVANIA

Allegheny Trail Alliance
P.O. Box 501, Latrobe
PA 15650
Tel: 888-282-2453
Email: atamail@atatrail.org
Web: www.atatrail.org
*Currently constructing the 152-mile
Great Allegheny Passage.*

SOUTH CAROLINA
Palmetto Conservation Foundation
1314 Lincoln St., PO Box 325
Columbia, SC 29201
Tel: 803-771-0870
Email: info@palmettoconservation.org
Web: www.palmettoconservation.org
*Conservation body that protects
natural and cultural resources.*

TENNESSEE
Tennessee Trails Association
P.O. Box 41446, Nashville
TN 37204-1446
Tel: 1-866-864-4537
Email:
    membership@TennesseeTrails.org
Web: www.tennesseetrails.org
*Promotes, builds, and maintains a
system of hiking trails in Tennessee.*

TEXAS
Lone Star Hiking Trail Club
113 Ben Drive, Houston, TX 77022
Tel: 713-410-8587
Email: trailguide@lshtclub.com
Web: www.lshtclub.com
*Dedicated to maintaining and
promoting hiking trails in Texas.*

UTAH
Mountain Trails Foundation
P.O. Box 754, Park City, UT 84060
Tel: 435-649-6839
Email: info@mountaintrails.org
Web: www.mountaintrails.org
*Promotes and preserves trails for
hikers in the Summit County area.*

VERMONT
Green Mountain Club
4711 Waterbury-Stowe Road
Waterbury Center, VT 05677
Tel: 802-244-7037
Email: gmc@greenmountainclub.org
Web: www.greenmountainclub.org
*Maintains the Long Trail System and
other trails in the state.*

VIRGINIA
Roanoke Appalachian Trail Club, Inc
P.O. Box 12282, Roanoke
VA 24024
Tel: 540-366-7780
Email: bob@peckmanjazz.com
Web: www.ratc.org
Organization of volunteers committed

*to preserving and promoting their
segment of the Appalachian Trail.*

WASHINGTON
Washington Trails Association
2019 Third Avenue, #100, Seattle
WA 98121
Tel: 206-625-1367
Email: elizabeth@wta.org
Web: www.wta.org
*Dedicated to promoting hiking
opportunities through education,
advocacy, and trail maintenance.*

WEST VIRGINIA
**West Virginia Scenic Trails
Association**
P.O. Box 4042, Charleston, WV 25364
Tel: 304-549-5702
Email:
    wvscenictrailsassn@yahoo.com
Web: www.wvnet.edu/wvsta/
*Nonprofit organization that aims to
develop and promote a system of
hiking trails in West Virginia.*

WISCONSIN
Ice Age Park and Trail Foundation
306 E. Wilson St., Lower Level,
Madison, WI 53703
Tel: 800-227-0046
Email: info@iceagetrail.org
Web: www.iceagetrail.org
*Maintains and protects the Ice
Age Trail, a 1,000-mile footpath
that follows Ice-Age formations in
Wisconsin.*

CANADIAN HIKING ORGANIZATIONS

Alpine Club of Canada
P.O. Box 804, Indian Flats Road
Canmore, AB, T1W 2T8
Tel: 403-678-3200
Email: info@AlpineClubofCanada.ca
Web: www.alpineclubofcanada.ca
*Organization with local club sections
that offers mountain adventures and
has an extensive system of huts.*

**Canadian National Parks
and Historic Sites**
Parks Canada, National Office, 25
Eddy Street, Gatineau, QC, K1A 0M5
Tel: 888-773-8888
Email: information@pc.gc.ca

Web: www.pc.gc.ca
*Holds an alphabetical list of Canada's
national and provincial parks.*

Go For Green
5480 Canotek Road, Unit 16
Gloucester, ON, K1J 9H6
Tel: 1-888-822-2848
Email: info@goforgreen.ca
Web: www.trailscanada.com
*Go For Green's "TrailsCanada"
program promotes community trail
initiatives across Canada. Includes
an online trail finder.*

Hike Canada/En Marche
16520 40th Avenue
Surrey, BC, V3S 0L2
Tel: 604-576-0403
Email: patharrison@shaw.ca
Web: www.nationaltrail.ca
*Hike Canada/En Marche has been
working on the vision of a footpath
across Canada for over 30 years.
Their website provides a history of
the National Hiking Trail and a list of
provincial organizations and trails.*

Out There
P.O. Box 64
Pte. Fortune, QC, J0P 1N0
Tel: 450-451-0884
Web: www.out-there.com
*Provides an extensive list
of backpacking and hiking
organizations in Canada, as well as
links to parks and trails.*

Trans Canada Trail
43 Westminster Avenue North
Montreal West, QC, H4X 1Y8
Tel: 1-800-465-3636
E-Mail: info@tctrail.ca
Web: www.tctrail.ca
*The website of the Trans Canada Trail
Foundation provides links to Trans
Canada Trail organizations in each
province and territory.*

Index

For Dorling Kindersley

Project Editor: Richard Gilbert; **Art Editor** Michael Duffy; **Managing Editor** Miranda Smith; **Managing Art Editor** Karen Self; **Art Director** Bryn Walls; **Publishing Director** Corinne Roberts; **DTP Designer** Karen Constanti; **Production Controller** Kevin Ward; **Illustrator** Julian Brown; **Map Illustrators** Michael Burgess and Iorwerth Watkins; **Studio Photography** Gary Ombler; **Location Photography** Gerard Brown.

Author's acknowledgments

The author would like to thank everyone from The Bridgewater Book Company and Dorling Kindersley who contributed to this book.

Publisher's acknowledgments

The Bridgewater Book Company would like to thank Ellis Brigham Ltd., Lowe Alpine, Peglers Expedition Advisors and Suppliers (www.peglers.co.uk), The North Face, and Yaktrax UK for the provision of outdoor clothing and equipment; the Alfriston Tennis Club & Camp Ground; and the following people for their contributions:

Project Editor Emily Casey Bailey; **Designer** Lisa McCormick; **Editors**: Alison Bolus, Sarah Doughty, Nicky Gyopari, Philippa Smith, Howard Spencer **Designers**: Kevin Knight, Ginny Zeal, Barbara Zuniga **Picture Researcher**: Maria Gibbs **Indexer**: Ann Barrett **Photoshoot Art Director**: Jo Grey **Prop Hunter**: Amy Jeavons **Models**: Natalie George, Andy Hillion, Miranda Hunt, Nicholas King, David McCormick, Hayley Miles, Paul Zimmerman

Dorling Kindersley would like to thank Dr. Viv Armstrong of the Red Cross, Jemima Dunne, and Jill Hamilton for their advice and help on the first aid section; Barbara Berger, Jennifer Crake, Lettie Luff, and John Searcy for assistance with the resources section; Jenny Siklos for Americanization, Karrimor, and Eadaoin Hutchinson at The North Face.

Picture Credits